ANNA LIFFEY

The River of Dublin

text

JOHN de COURCY

illustrations

STEPHEN CONLIN

THE O'BRIEN PRESS
DUBLIN

First published 1988 by The O'Brien Press Ltd.,
20 Victoria Road, Rathgar, Dublin 6, Ireland.

Copyright ©.

British Library Cataloguing in Publication Data
de Courcy, John
Anna Liffey : the river of Dublin.
1. (County) Dublin. Liffey River, to 1988
I. Title II. Conlin, Stephen
941.8'3
ISBN 0-86278-169-8
ISBN 0-86278-168-X panoramic view

10 9 8 7 6 5 4 3 2 1

Acknowledgements: Hamish Hamilton Ltd. for an extract
on page 18 from 'The Great Hunger' by Cecil
Woodham-Smith.
Society of Authors for an extract on page 57 from *Ulysses*
by James Joyce.

Book and cover design: Michael O'Brien
Typesetting and origination: The O'Brien Press.
Set in Schoolbook 10/12.5.
Printing: Irish Elsevier Printers, Shannon

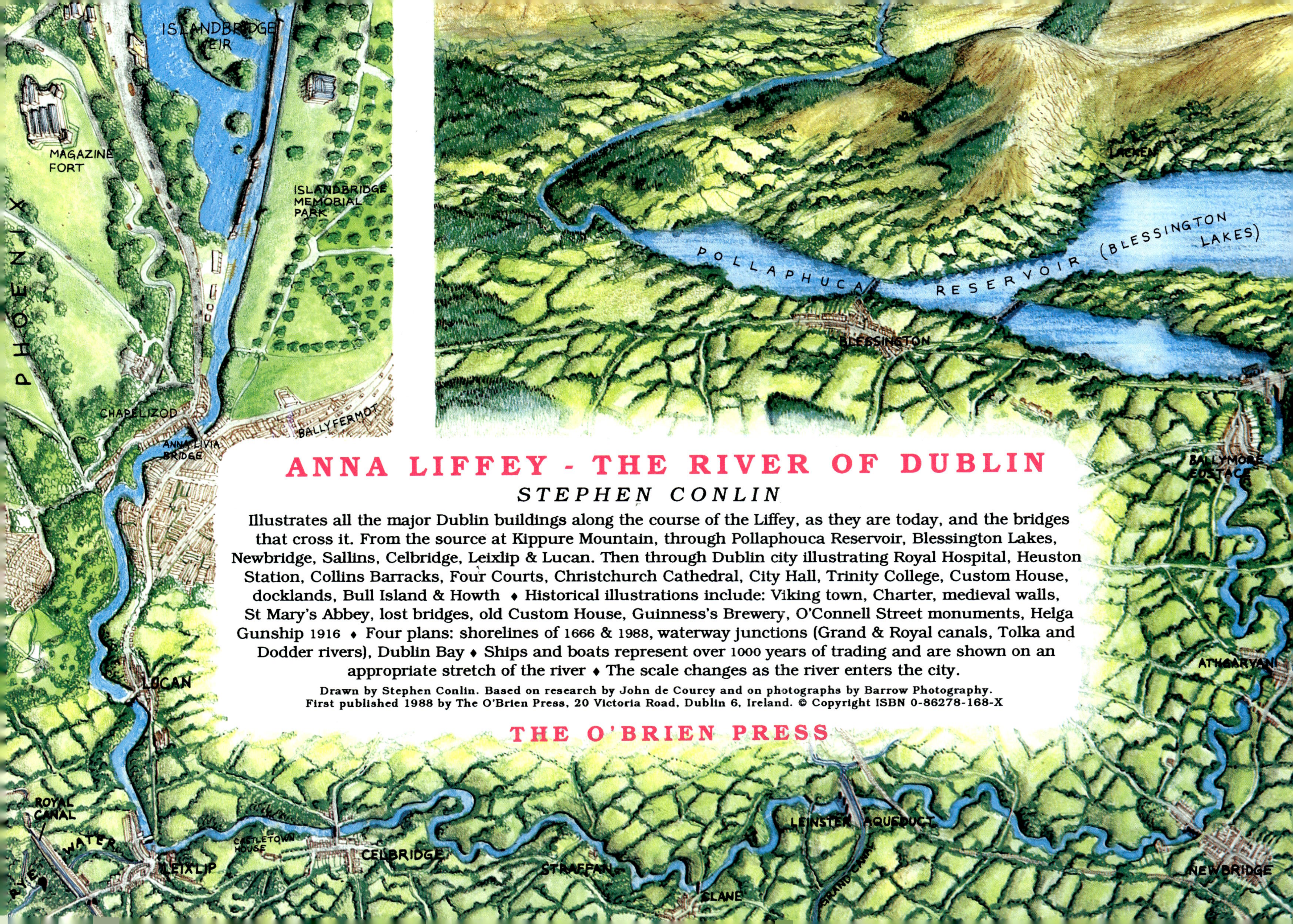

ANNA LIFFEY - THE RIVER OF DUBLIN

STEPHEN CONLIN

Illustrates all the major Dublin buildings along the course of the Liffey, as they are today, and the bridges that cross it. From the source at Kippure Mountain, through Pollaphouca Reservoir, Blessington Lakes, Newbridge, Sallins, Celbridge, Leixlip & Lucan. Then through Dublin city illustrating Royal Hospital, Heuston Station, Collins Barracks, Four Courts, Christchurch Cathedral, City Hall, Trinity College, Custom House, docklands, Bull Island & Howth ♦ Historical illustrations include: Viking town, Charter, medieval walls, St Mary's Abbey, lost bridges, old Custom House, Guinness's Brewery, O'Connell Street monuments, Helga Gunship 1916 ♦ Four plans: shorelines of 1666 & 1988, waterway junctions (Grand & Royal canals, Tolka and Dodder rivers), Dublin Bay ♦ Ships and boats represent over 1000 years of trading and are shown on an appropriate stretch of the river ♦ The scale changes as the river enters the city.

Drawn by Stephen Conlin. Based on research by John de Courcy and on photographs by Barrow Photography.
First published 1988 by The O'Brien Press, 20 Victoria Road, Dublin 6, Ireland. © Copyright ISBN 0-86278-168-X

THE O'BRIEN PRESS

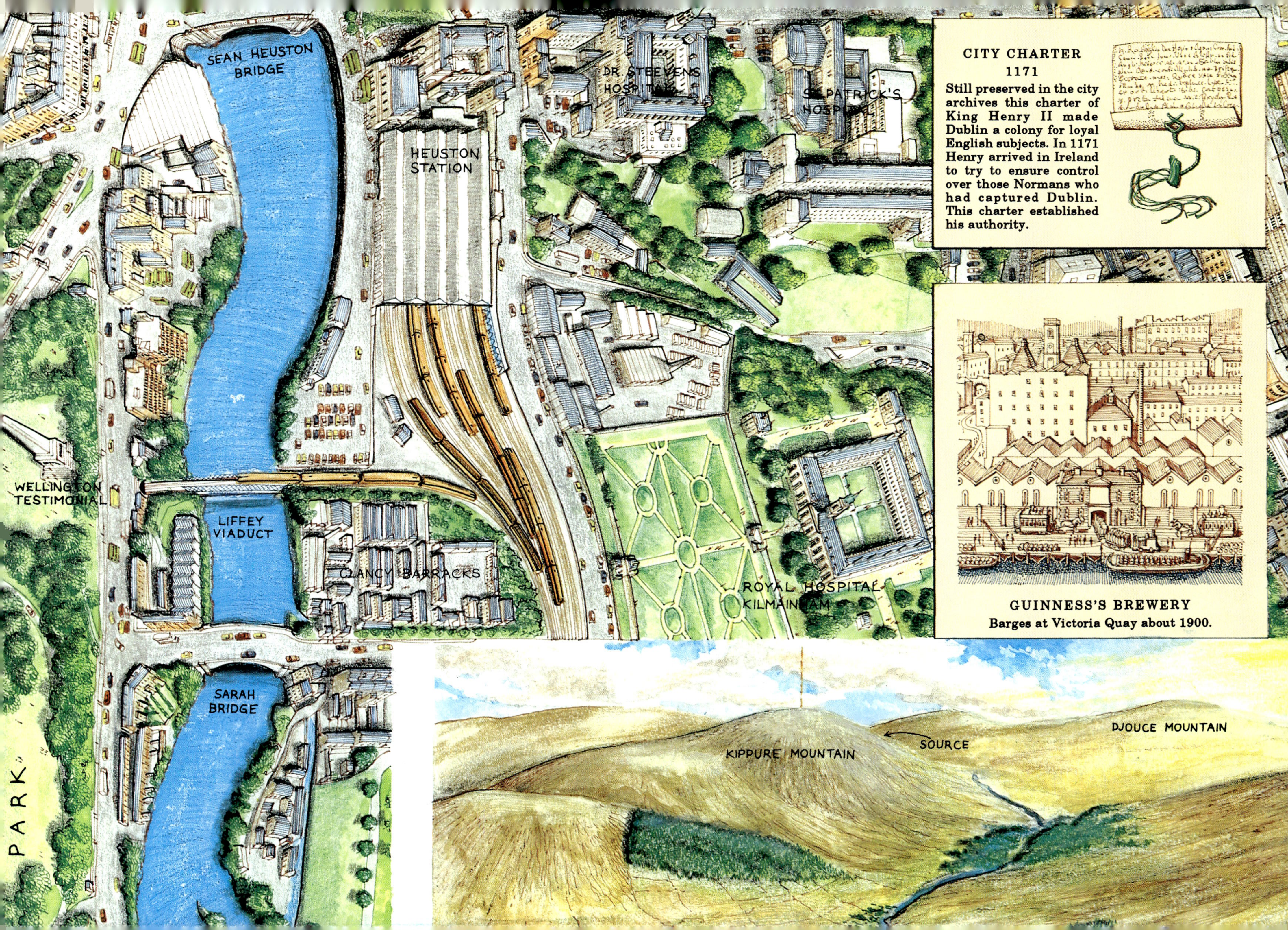

CITY CHARTER
1171

Still preserved in the city archives this charter of King Henry II made Dublin a colony for loyal English subjects. In 1171 Henry arrived in Ireland to try to ensure control over those Normans who had captured Dublin. This charter established his authority.

GUINNESS'S BREWERY
Barges at Victoria Quay about 1900.

COLLINS BARRACKS
CROPPIES ACRE
WOLFE TONE QUAY
RORY O'MORE BRIDGE
VICTORIA QUAY
OLD GUINNESS BARGES (1873-1961)
GUINNESS'S BREWERY
FRANK SHERWIN BRIDGE
LOST BRIDGES
Typical early timber bridge
'Old Bridge of Dublin' (1428-1816)
Ormonde Bridge (1684-1802)
Essex Bridge 1755, which replaced the bridge built by Jervis in 1678.
GEORGE I AND ESSEX BRIDGE
An equestrian statue of George I by the elder Van Nost stood on Essex Bridge from 1722 to 1753. It was then taken down and in the nineteenth century stood outside the Mansion House. Sold in 1937 to the Barber Institute, where it now stands.
VIKING HOUSES
Typical post and wattle houses built by the Vikings who came to Dublin in the 9th century. From excavations at High St. and Wood Quay.
TOWERS AND WALLS
Only the Record Tower of Dublin Castle remains of the thirty-six towers set into the old town walls.
GUNBOAT HELGA AND 1916
The Helga is shown outside the Custom House as British forces attempt to bombard Liberty Hall during the Easter Rising. She was also used to carry 'Black and Tan' troops around Ireland. Later remamed Muirchu and used during the 1922 Civil War.

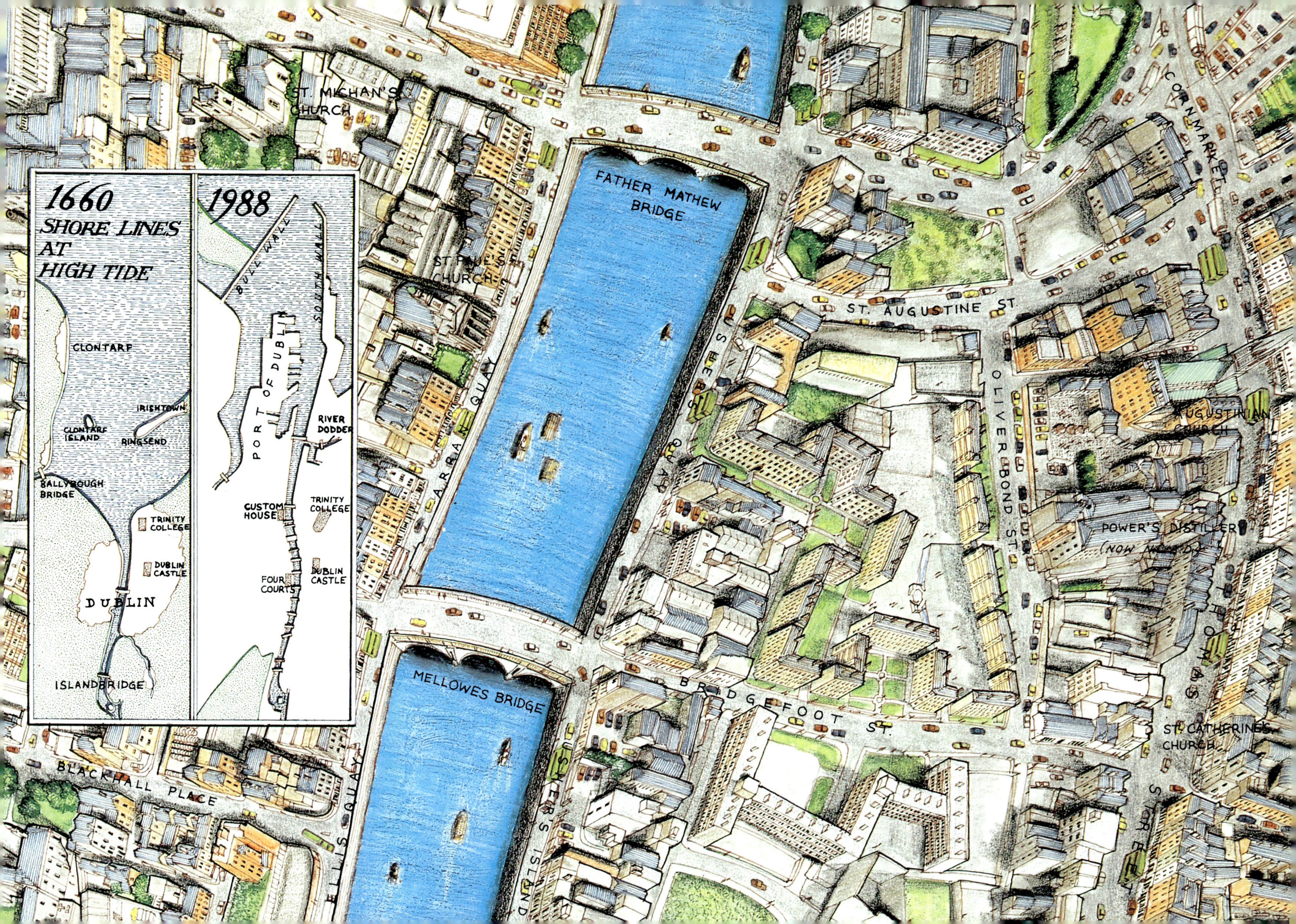

1660
SHORE LINES
AT
HIGH TIDE
CLONTARF
CLONTARF ISLAND
IRISHTOWN
RINGSEND
BALLYBOUGH BRIDGE
TRINITY COLLEGE
DUBLIN CASTLE
DUBLIN
ISLANDBRIDGE
1988
PORT OF DUBLIN
BULL WALL
SOUTH WALL
RIVER DODDER
CUSTOM HOUSE
TRINITY COLLEGE
FOUR COURTS
DUBLIN CASTLE
ST. MICHAN'S CHURCH
ST. PAUL'S CHURCH
FATHER MATHEW BRIDGE
ARRAN QUAY
USHER'S QUAY
CORN MARKET
ST. AUGUSTINE ST.
OLIVER BOND ST.
AUGUSTINIAN CHURCH
POWER'S DISTILLERY
(NOW NEW ...)
MELLOWES BRIDGE
USHER'S ISLAND
BRIDGEFOOT ST.
ST. CATHERINE'S CHURCH
BLACKHALL PLACE
ELLIS QUAY

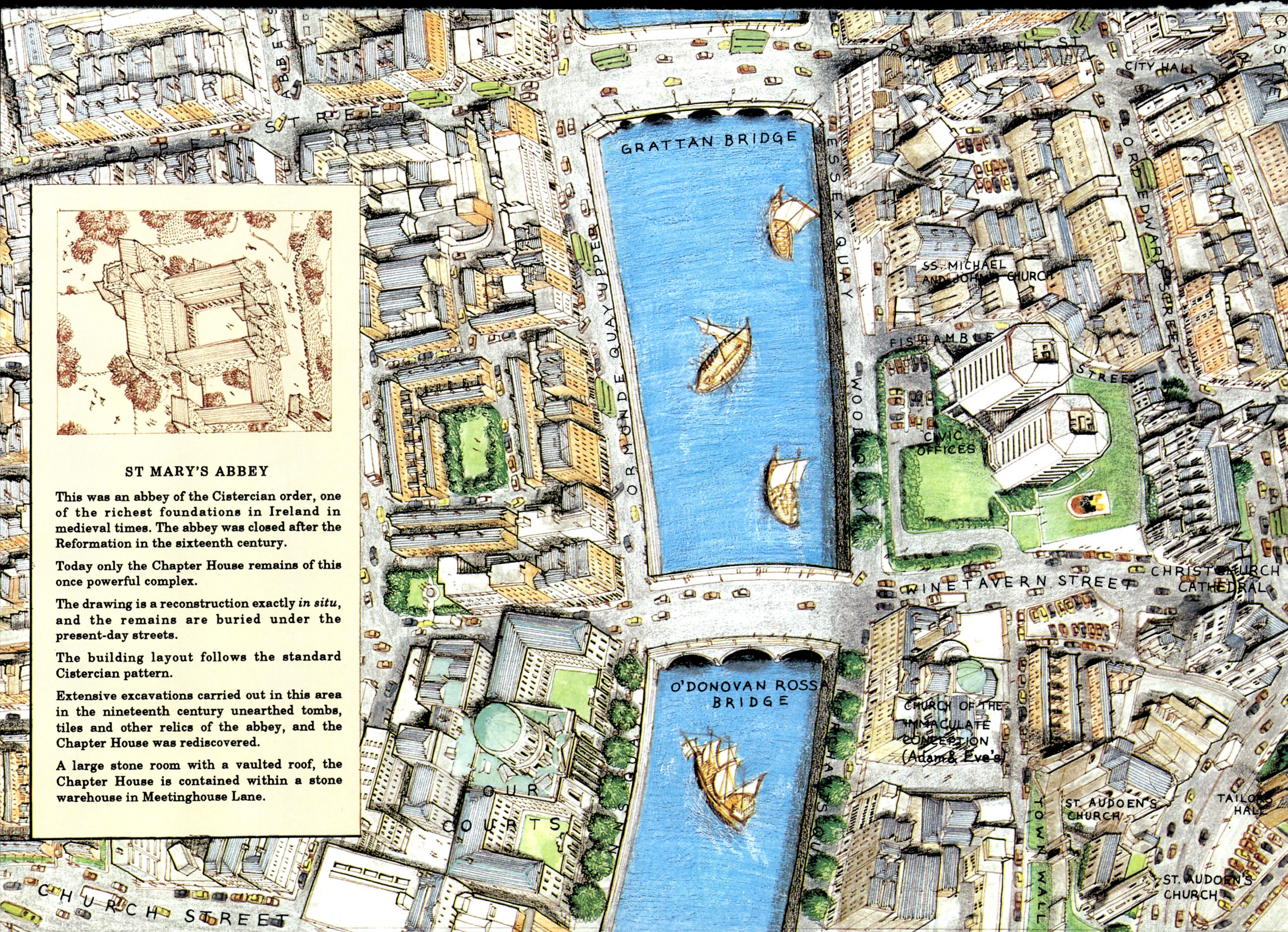

ST MARY'S ABBEY

This was an abbey of the Cistercian order, one
of the richest foundations in Ireland in
medieval times. The abbey was closed after the
Reformation in the sixteenth century.

Today only the Chapter House remains of this
once powerful complex.

The drawing is a reconstruction exactly in situ,
and the remains are buried under the
present-day streets.

The building layout follows the standard
Cistercian pattern.

Extensive excavations carried out in this area
in the nineteenth century unearthed tombs,
tiles and other relics of the abbey, and the
Chapter House was rediscovered.

A large stone room with a vaulted roof, the
Chapter House is contained within a stone
warehouse in Meetinghouse Lane.

ABBEY ST
CASTLE STREET
CITY HALL
CARE ST REE
GRATTAN BRIDGE
ESSEX QUAY
OR DE DWARF STREET
SS. MICHAEL AND JOHN'S CHURCH
ORMONDE QUAY UPPER
FISHAMBLE STREET
WOOD QUAY
CIVIC OFFICES
INNS QUAY
WINE TAVERN STREET
CHRIST CHURCH CATHEDRAL
O'DONOVAN ROSS BRIDGE
APPLE STREET
CHURCH OF THE IMMACULATE CONCEPTION (Adam & Eve's)
FOUR COURTS
TOWN WALL
ST. AUDOEN'S CHURCH
TAILORS HALL
CHURCH STREET
ST. AUDOEN'S CHURCH

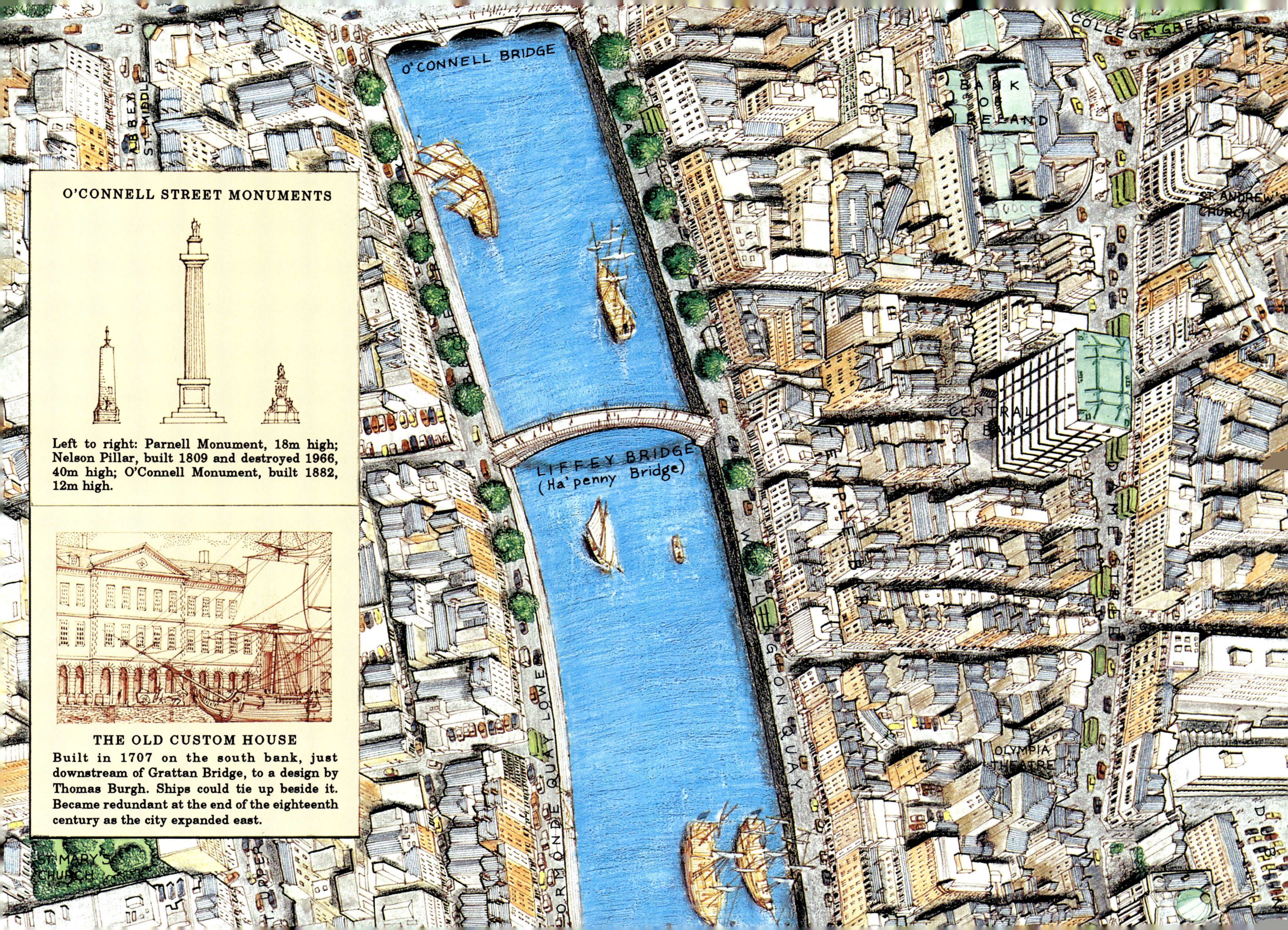

O'CONNELL STREET MONUMENTS
Left to right: Parnell Monument, 18m high; Nelson Pillar, built 1809 and destroyed 1966, 40m high; O'Connell Monument, built 1882, 12m high.
THE OLD CUSTOM HOUSE
Built in 1707 on the south bank, just downstream of Grattan Bridge, to a design by Thomas Burgh. Ships could tie up beside it. Became redundant at the end of the eighteenth century as the city expanded east.
ABBEY ST. MIDDLE
O'CONNELL BRIDGE
COLLEGE GREEN
BANK OF IRELAND
ST. ANDREW'S CHURCH
CENTRAL BANK
LIFFEY BRIDGE (Ha'penny Bridge)
ORMONDE QUAY LOWER
WELLINGTON QUAY
OLYMPIA THEATRE
ST. MARY'S CHURCH

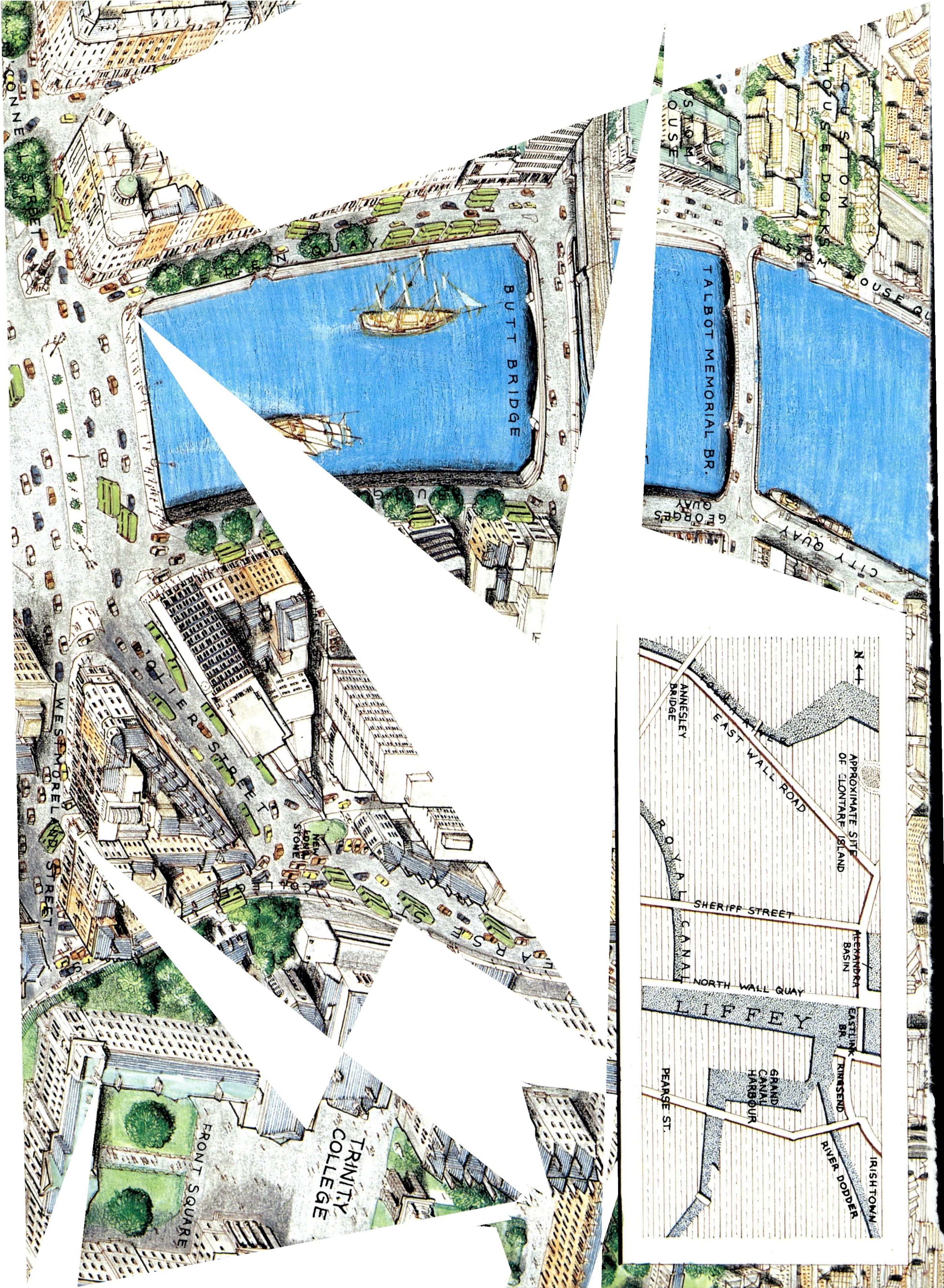
O'CONNELL STREET
BUTT BRIDGE
TALBOT MEMORIAL BR.
CUSTOM HOUSE DOCK
CUSTOM HOUSE QUAY
CUSTOM HOUSE
GEORGES QUAY
CITY QUAY
WESTMORELAND STREET
D'OLIER STREET
COLLEGE STREET
NASSAU STREET
TRINITY COLLEGE
FRONT SQUARE
NELSON'S PILLAR
N
ANNESLEY BRIDGE
EAST WALL ROAD
APPROXIMATE SITE OF CLONTARF ISLAND
ROYAL CANAL
SHERIFF STREET
ALEXANDRA BASIN
NORTH WALL QUAY
LIFFEY
EASTLINK BR.
RINGSEND
GRAND CANAL HARBOUR
PEARSE ST.
RIVER DODDER
IRISHTOWN

ANNA LIFFEY
The River of Dublin

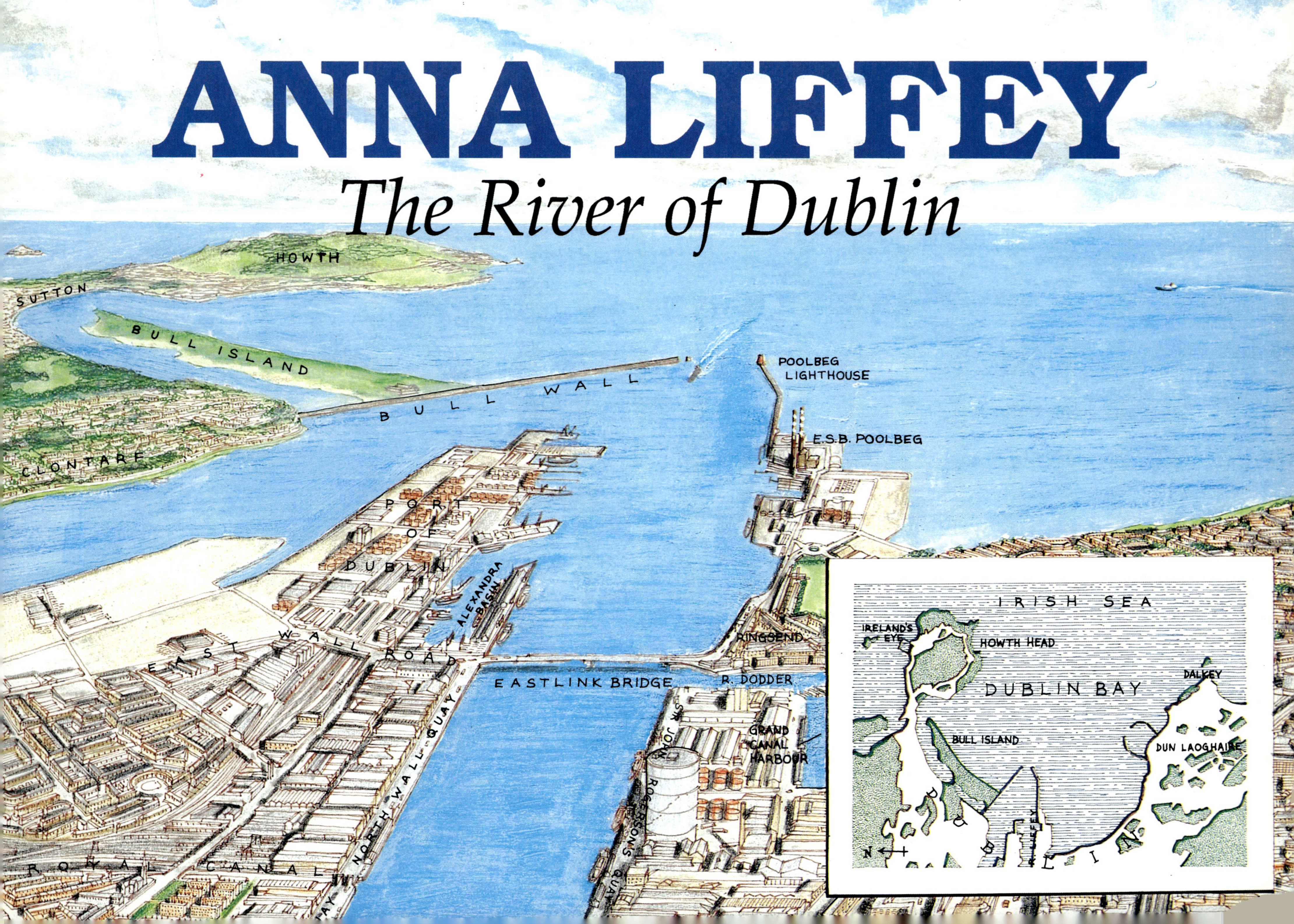

CONTENTS

Introduction page 5

1 Names for the River Liffey 6

2 The Source of the Liffey and the River in County Wicklow 6

3 Pollaphuca Bridge 6

4 The Liffey in County Kildare 6

5 The Leinster Aquaduct 8

6 The Rye Water River 8

7 The Liffey Passes through County Dublin and Enters the City 9

8 The Ancient Shore Line of the Liffey 10

9 The Weir and Islands at Islandbridge 11

10 Kilmehanoc Ford 11

11 Kilmainham and Sarah Bridges 12

12 The Royal Hospital at Kilmainham 13

13 Liffey Viaduct 14

14 The River Camac 15

15 Heuston Railway Station 15

16 The Quays in General 15

17 The South Quays 16

18 The North Quays 16

19 Sean Heuston Bridge 17

20 Frank Sherwin Bridge 17

21 Collins Barracks 18

22 Soyer's Food Kitchen 18

23 Gravel Walk Slip and Slips in General 19

24 The River Ferries 19

25 Rory O'More Bridge 20

26 Richmond Guard Tower 21

27 Moira House 22

28 Usher's Island 23

29 Mellowes Bridge 23

30 Ath Cliath 23

31 Father Mathew Bridge 24

32 The Four Courts and Saint Saviour's Priory 24

33 O'Donovan Rossa Bridge 26

34 Ormonde Bridge 27

35 Towers on the River 27

36 Wood Quay 28

37 Gunpowder Explosion at Wood Quay 30

38 The Bradogue River 31

39 Saint Mary's Abbey 31

40 The River Poddle 32

41 The Old Custom House 33

42 Grattan Bridge 34

43 Equestrian Statue of King George 1 at Essex Bridge 35

44 Steadfast Dick 36

45 The Ha'penny Bridge 36

46 Hoggen Green 36

47 The Battle of Hoggen Green 38

48 The Bagnio Slip 39

49 O'Connell Bridge 40

50 The Bank of Ireland on College Green 41

51 Trinity College and All Hallows Priory 42

52 The River Stein 43

53 Butt Bridge 43

54 Loopline Bridge 43

55

56 Talbot Memorial Bridge 44

57 The Custom House Docks 45

58 Lazers Hill 45

59 The Hibernian Marine School 46

60 The East Wall 47

61 The Canal Docks 48

62 The River Dodder 49

63 The New Port 49

64 Ringsend 50

65 Eastlink Bridge 50

66 The Pigeonhouse 52

67 The Pools in the Estuary 53

68 Clontarf Island 54

69 The North Bull and Bull Island 55

70 The South Bull 56

71 The Eastern Franchises 57

72 The Draught of Turleyhydes 57

73 The Wreck of the *Prince of Wales* and the *Rochdale* 57

74 The Great South Wall 58

75 The Poolbeg Lighthouse 59

Index 61

INTRODUCTION

A river in a wilderness is for the geologist, the botanist, the naturalist. A river in a developed environment is for the geographer, the historian, the legislator. In both settings, the river is also for the people who live beside it, who observe and experience its nature, who sense that a place with a river will always have qualities that only the river can give.

Stephen Conlin's drawing suggests various images of the Liffey as it flows from Kippure to the sea. It is to help deepen some of those images that these notes are offered. They are, of necessity, selective. They describe generally what has happened or been made, and only rarely do they touch on what has from time to time been proposed but never achieved. They occasionally offer opinions and speculate, hopefully in a spirit happy to bow to authority when authority proves its point.

A bibliography is not included. Many sources have been consulted and their assistance is gratefully acknowledged. It would be fitting to mention such names, not cited in the text, as Ball, Blacker, Craig, Curtis, Dalton, Gilbert, Haliday, Harris, Healy, Martin, Semple, Wallace, Walsh, Warburton, and Weston Joyce, if one were not conscious of omitting others. The superbly edited volumes of the *Calendar of the Ancient Records of Dublin* have been invaluable, and a debt of thanks is due to the late Frank Murphy for his kindness in providing access to these. The fifty-year collection of the *Dublin Historical Record* and the exhibits in the Civic Museum are important sources. The courtesy of the National Library, the Public Records office, the City Archives, the Port and Docks Board, University College, Dublin and the Institution of Engineers of Ireland has been much appreciated, as have the facilities generously offered by the British Library, the National Maritime Museum in Greenwich, and the Hatfield Collection.

The author is grateful to many people for numerous conversations graciously endured, and he thanks his wife, Sheila, for her patience and care in preparing these notes for publication.

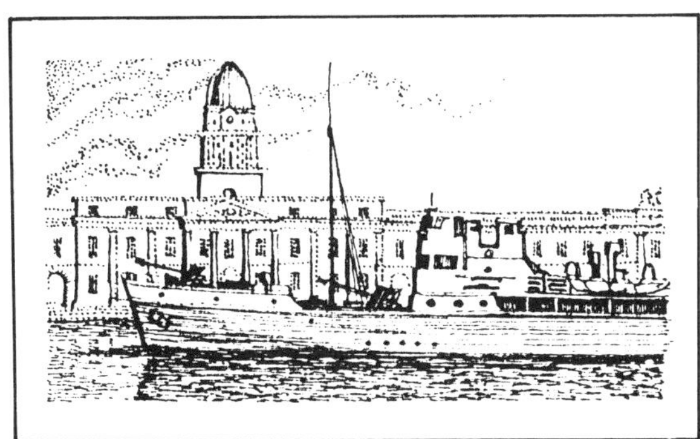

1. NAMES FOR THE RIVER LIFFEY

It would appear that at one time parts of the plain of Kildare were known as the plain of Liffe. The river that flowed through these parts was the river of Liffe, perhaps Abha or Abhann Liffe, or, as it could have become in an Anglicised version, Avon Liffey. Through the centuries the name appears in many forms — in public records, charters, deeds and maps — and, in the absence of a single recognised spelling, these names may well have reflected the sounds that individual scribes heard. Some of these forms follow. They suggest Irish, English, French and Latin influences.

The name of the river is Alyffy, Amliffy, Amplifee, Ampnlyffy, Analiffey, Aneliffe, Aniliffy, Anlyffe, Anna liffe, Anna Liffey, Annaliffy, Annalyffy, Anneliffi, Annelyffee, Anne lyffy, Annlyffy, Antlyffie, Auenelith, Auenlif, Aunlyffe, Avanalith, Avanlith, Aveneliffy, Avenelit, Avenelith, Avenesliz, Avenliffey, Avenlithe, Avenlyf, Aveyn Liffy, Avon Liffey, Liffe, Liffee, Liffey, Liffie, Lybinum, Lyffie, Lyffye, River of Dublin, Ruirteach, Ruirtech.

While the formal name now is Liffey, the name Anna Liffey was retained in some official documents until relatively recently; and this form would have led to James Joyce's Anna Livia Plurabelle.

Another term applied to the river in old records was Ruirtech or Ruirteach. This surely suggests an adjective rather than a primary name, and it is said that it did in fact mean "furious" or "raging". Such a description would have been appropriate because of the flash flooding that could convert a placid river without warning into a destructive torrent in a matter of hours. This quality of the Liffey was not brought under control until the river was harnessed earlier this century by dams in Pollaphuca, Golden Falls and Leixlip.

2. THE SOURCE OF THE LIFFEY AND THE RIVER IN COUNTY WICKLOW

The River Liffey rises in County Wicklow on a shoulder of Kippure, some three kilometres southeast of the summit of the mountain. The road from Glencree to the Sally Gap crosses the infant stream about one kilometre south of the entrance to the Kippure TV transmitter station. A short walk east from the road, perhaps 300 metres, the first trickles of water flow from a rim of peat hags, and this is the source of the river. This point, as the crow might fly, is only twenty-three kilometres from Poolbeg lighthouse where the Liffey finally enters Dublin Bay. It is interesting to contrast this distance with the actual length of the river which, with its great loop through Kildare, is about 110 kilometres.

It might fairly be argued that the Kings River, the first tributary of the Liffey, is equally its source. The Kings River has its own scattered beginnings at the Three Lakes of Table Mountain near Art O'Neill's grave, and up past Glenbride under the south side of Mullacleevaun and the west side of Tonlagee. It drains the whole valley lying west of the Wicklow Gap before turning north to join the Liffey at a confluence now submerged in the Blessington reservoir. The lengths of the two rivers down to this junction are about the same. The ascendancy of one over the other is lost in history.

3. POLLAPHUCA BRIDGE

In the late eighteenth century, there was already a bridge crossing the Liffey near Pollaphuca on the road from Dublin through Blessington to Baltinglass. Whether because of the alignment of this bridge or because of its condition, a new structure was found necessary and the present Pollaphuca bridge with its battlement parapets was built, to a design by the Scottish-born engineer, Alexander Nimo, prior to the year 1830. The pointed arch of the bridge was a feature favoured by Nimmo, who lived and worked in Ireland from 1811 until his death in Dublin in 1832, being responsible for many important works, particularly in Connaught.

This quite daring bridge, with the road crossing roughly forty-five metres above the level of the river was probably the highest road bridge structure in Ireland at the time of its construction. Indeed, it remains among the highest today. A feature of the bridge is that it is approached from the south by an arched viaduct that carries the road over a dry valley beside the river.

4. THE LIFFEY IN COUNTY KILDARE

The Liffey literally tumbles into County Kildare through the bridge at Pollaphuca. It is then guided through the hydro-electric complex of Pollaphuca and Golden Falls and sent off through Ballymore Eustace to follow its own ancient course across Kildare, not to be restrained again until it reaches Leixlip at the far end of the county where it is once more put to the work of making electricity.

The river meanders through Kildare, twisting this way and that as though loath to leave the quiet of the countryside for the fuss of Dublin. Old stone bridges, placid in their age, cross it at intervals. At Harristown we find the New Bridge, built by John La Touche in 1788, six arches in the span, with one of Victoria's post boxes only a few hundred yards away, now painted green. And when that crossing was new, one suspects that the bridge at Carragh, ten kilometres to the north by air, and twice as far by water, was already venerable, with its six small, unequal arches and less than three metres between its parapets.

As one approaches Droichead Nua, the form of the arches suggests from a distance that some new influence has shaped the river crossing. And so it is no surprise to find that the town known only as New Bridge Inn in the eighteenth century had received in 1936 its second (or perhaps its third) new bridge since then — and this time as three large spans of reinforced concrete. A visit to Kilcullen will suggest how exquisite the old Liffey bridge there was, with its six high stone arches; but view it from downstream to see its original form.

A feature not often explored in Kildare is the ancient Woolpack Road, the pack-horse route, that goes east from the Curragh to Rathcoole. This road, in the old days, crossed the Liffey by a ford at Athgarvan. Today it crosses by a five-arch stone bridge, itself now old, with parapets so low as to be little more than high kerbs; but the position of the ford alongside remains quite clear.

The accession of Queen Victoria to the throne in 1837 was celebrated in many ways, including the building of a three-arched stone bridge across the Liffey not far from Naas. When the Queen's son Edward

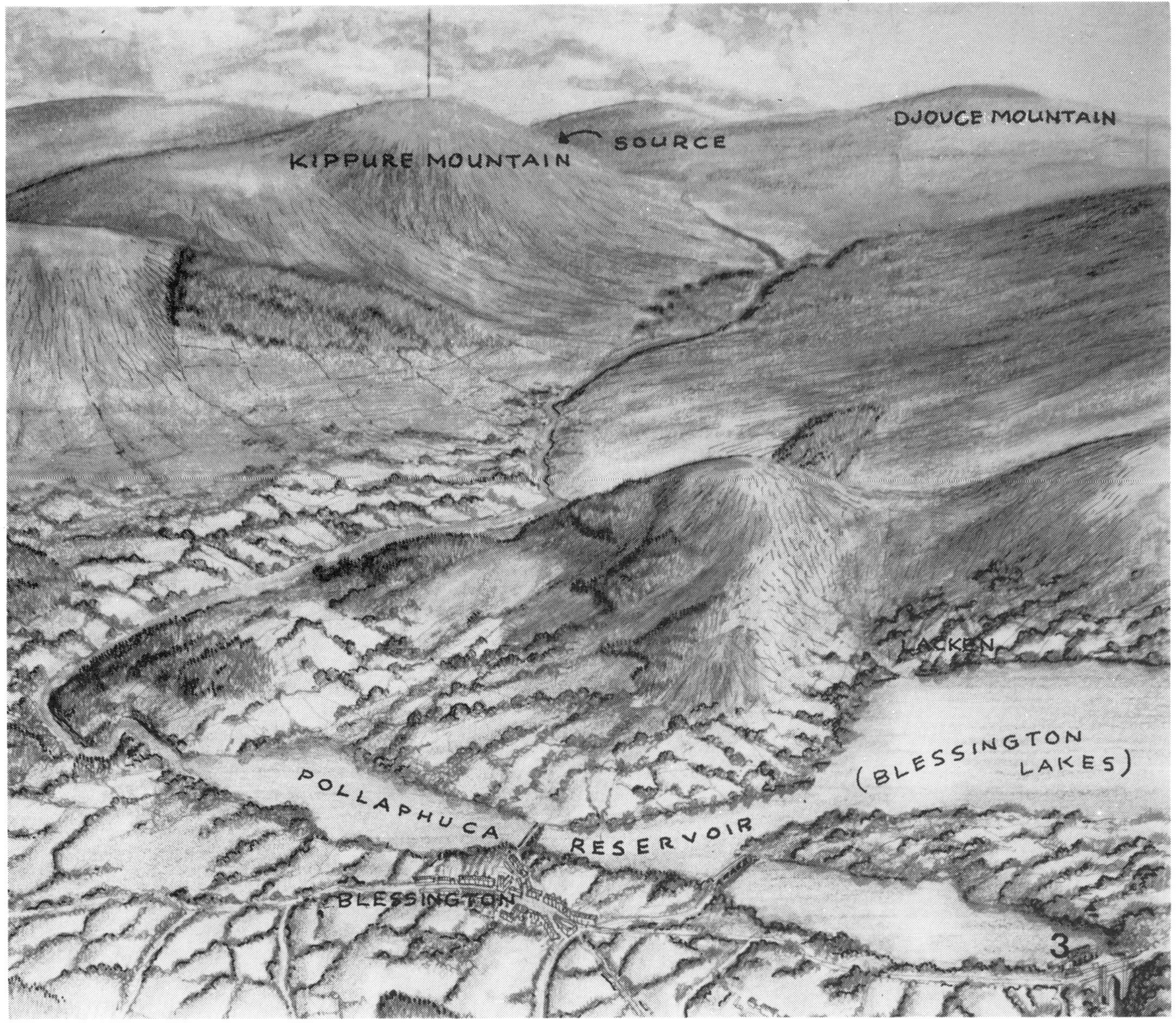

married the Danish princess Alexandra, the occasion was again marked by a three-arched bridge over the Liffey in Kildare, this time near Clane. Plaques on these two bridges offer the single names of Victoria on the one and Alexandra on the other, cut in stone with the dates of the bridges, 1837 and 1864. There may be some significance, whether from famine or otherwise, in the fact that the first name has almost been obliterated by chiselling away the letters, while the second remains pristine.

Theobald Wolfe Tone, who died in 1798, lies buried at Bodenstown between the two bridges, and near another, named Millicent Bridge.

Passing Straffan with its public and private bridges, the Liffey briefly recalls Swift and Vanessa, flows on through Celbridge, under its strange bridge of five arches with the eccentric hump, and so on towards the long man-made lake above Leixlip. It was here, as the town's name acknowledges, that the salmon at one time leaped, but no longer. Now they are lifted safely and efficiently, though perhaps less nobly, in a tube.

The last gesture that Kildare makes to the Liffey is to offer it in tribute the Rye Water River that flows in from the north to join the main stream just as it starts out again on its own course into County Dublin from below the power station dam.

5. THE LEINSTER AQUEDUCT

About one kilometre west of Sallins, the Grand Canal sends off a branch to the south through Naas to end rather unexpectedly at Corbally, not far from Athgarvan. Just west of this junction, the main canal is carried across the River Liffey on the Leinster Aqueduct. In this unusual type of structure, the canal, with its towpath and a roadway, passes high above the river, thus avoiding the necessity for locking down one side of the valley and up the other.

The river crossing at the Leinster Aqueduct consists of five stone arches. The view from upstream presents the strange proportions that arise from quite small arches and the massive superstructure that is required to contain the channel for the canal. This aqueduct was designed by Richard Evans and built around 1780.

6. THE RYE WATER RIVER

The Rye Water River, one of the chief tributaries of the Liffey, joins it from the north at Leixlip. It rises west of Kilcock and flows east along the county boundary between Kildare and Meath. It passes north of Maynooth and then enters the lands of Carton, former home of the Earls of Kildare, where it is dammed to form an artificial lake. Here it is joined by other streams to emerge as a sizeable river, deemed navigable in earlier times for small commercial boats.

About a kilometre west of Leixlip the Royal Canal is carried over the Rye Water at a height of some twenty-five metres, in what is fairly described as an

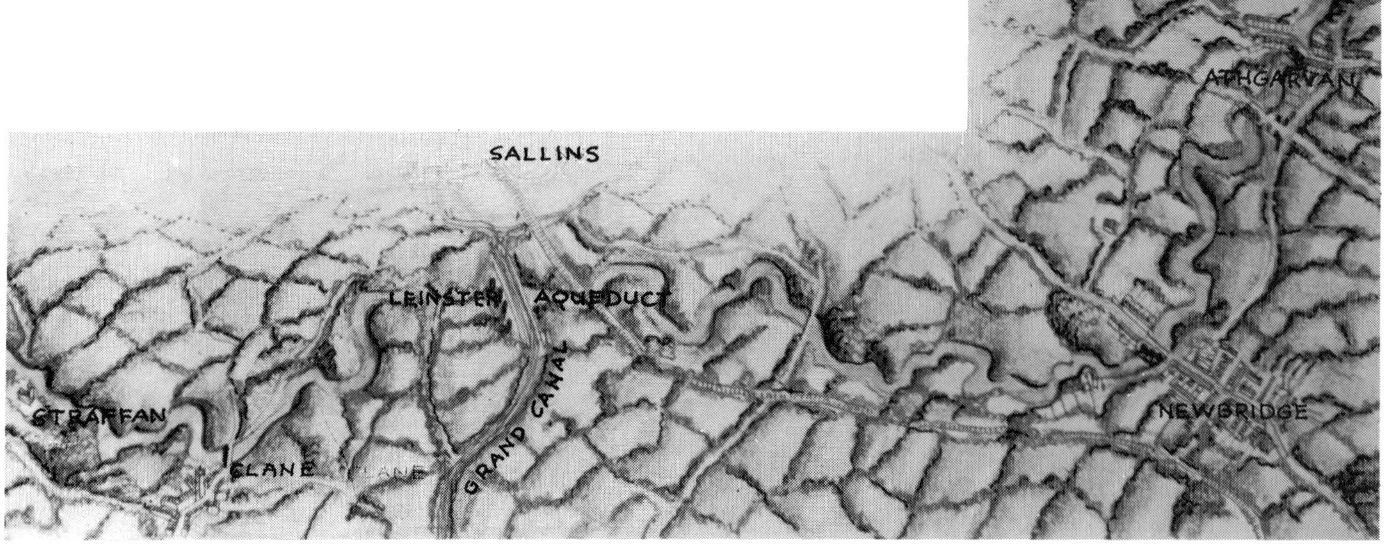

aqueduct. It is unusual however in that the aqueduct in this instance consists of an immense earthen embankment about 300 metres long, with the canal on top and the river passing through below in a stone arched tunnel. This work was begun in 1791 but, due to its very size and to problems of flooding, was not completed until 1796. Fifty years later, in 1846, the Midland Great Western Railway line to Mullingar was laid beside the canal, sharing the same aqueduct or an extension of it.

Passing through the town of Leixlip, the Rye Water flows under the main street in a stone arch of several small spans. An unusual feature here is the retention of the projecting stones on the uprights, probably used to support the timber frames on which the actual arches were built.

7. THE LIFFEY PASSES THROUGH COUNTY DUBLIN AND ENTERS THE CITY

The Liffey enters County Dublin at the Leixlip Bridge and flows with little meandering through Lucan and Chapelizod into Dublin. The high and elegant three-span stone arched bridge at Leixlip carries no indication of its name or age, and manifests itself to passing traffic only by the right-angled bends in the road at both ends and by the visual discouragement of its somewhat displaced west railing.

In Lucan, the river is joined by the little Griffeen River which flows in from the south under a small but quite complex stone bridge which was "built by Agm Vesey for ye public in ye yer 1773" (Agm is an abbreviation of the name Agmondisham); and the Liffey then flows under what is arguably the finest stone bridge in its entire course, carrying the road leading towards Clonsilla and the north. This bridge, with its great single span of about thirty-six metres and elaborate cast iron balusters, gives no indication of its name or age, other than that the metal balusters were made by the Phoenix Iron Works of Dublin in 1814. The bridge has been a little injured in its appearance by the raising of the roadway near both ends of the arch to improve the gradient, but its overall appearance, especially in the context of the high weir and falls just upstream, is splendid.

The comparative seclusion of the Liffey in this stretch may be gauged from the fact that in the eight kilometres of road past the Strawberry Beds to Chapelizod there is no public bridge across the river, and only one private crossing, a metal bridge quite fine in concept but now disused and deteriorating. About the Strawberry Beds themselves, named for the simple reason that this fruit was grown extensively here, Weston Joyce records that the area was formerly very popular for Sunday excursions from the city. The fare by horse-drawn car from Carlisle Bridge was 3d and "it was not an infrequent sight to see a long procession of these vehicles, amid blinding

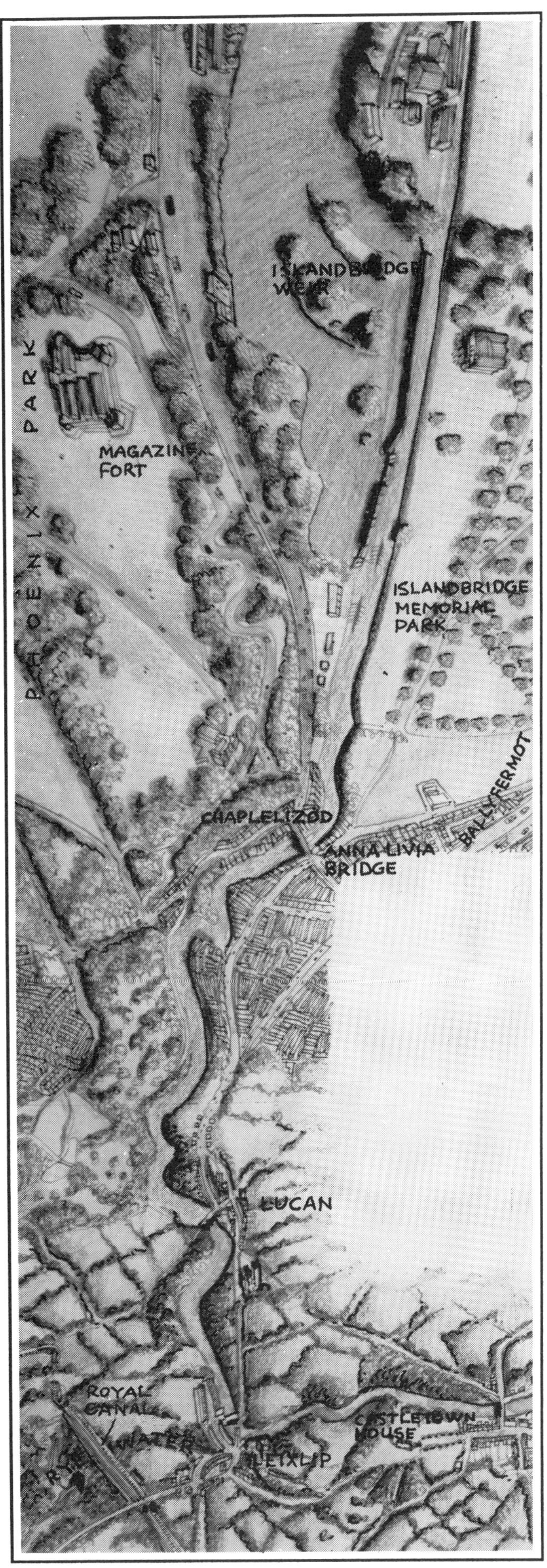

clouds of dust, extending the whole way from Parkgate Street to Knockmaroon."

As the Liffey flows into Chapelizod, a weir forms a
large mill-race that makes an island on which industry has flourished for at least 150 years. The main
stream is crossed by a four-span stone arched bridge,
unusual in having two large central spans and two
much smaller end spans. This bridge, formerly
Chapelizod Bridge, now has incised upon its parapet
"Renamed 1982 to mark the centenary of James
Joyce's birth. Dublin Corporation" and also "Anna
Livia. James Joyce 1882-1941." No reference is made
to *Finnegans Wake*, although this work probably suggested Chapelizod as a place to remember its author.

From here a broad and slow-flowing stretch of the
Liffey, held up by the weir at Islandbridge, passes several of the city boat clubs and is extensively used by
them for training. Here also the river skirts the northern edge of the rather forlorn Islandbridge Memorial
Park, designed by Sir Edwin Lutyens to commemorate Irishmen who died in the war of 1914-1918. The
park was completed under the direction of the Office
of Public Works and not formally opened until 1940.

8. THE ANCIENT SHORE LINE OF THE LIFFEY

In the year 800, before man influenced the shape
of the river, the water level in the Liffey rose and fell
with the tide to very much the same levels as it does
today. The tide reached up to somewhere between
Islandbridge and Chapelizod, and the level of the
water was of course also influenced by fluctuations in
the amount of rain falling in the Liffey basin generally. Allowing that flash flooding, for which the river
was notorious until about forty years ago, was a rare
occurrence, the chief factor in determining the effec-
tive outline of the river was the high-water level at
ordinary spring tides.

The line of this high-water mark varied little from
800 to 1600. During these eight hundred years, except
for the formation of Wood Quay and the walling or
embankment of small parts of the north shore by the
monks of Saint Mary's Abbey and Saint Saviour's
Priory, the high-tide shore line would have been, near
the sea, a shingly bank with sea weed and shell, and,
further upstream, low sedgy banks bounding rough
grass or scrub. Here and there, creeks and rivulets
would have made breaks in the banks and some of
these would have given access to tidal or marshy pools
lying behind the banks and perhaps quite some distance from the river.

It is of interest to follow this high-tide shore line,
although it must be borne in mind that the details are
to some degree speculative.

From Dollymount to Fairview the shore generally
followed the present Clontarf Road. There was no Bull
Island, no port and no East Wall, so at high tide the

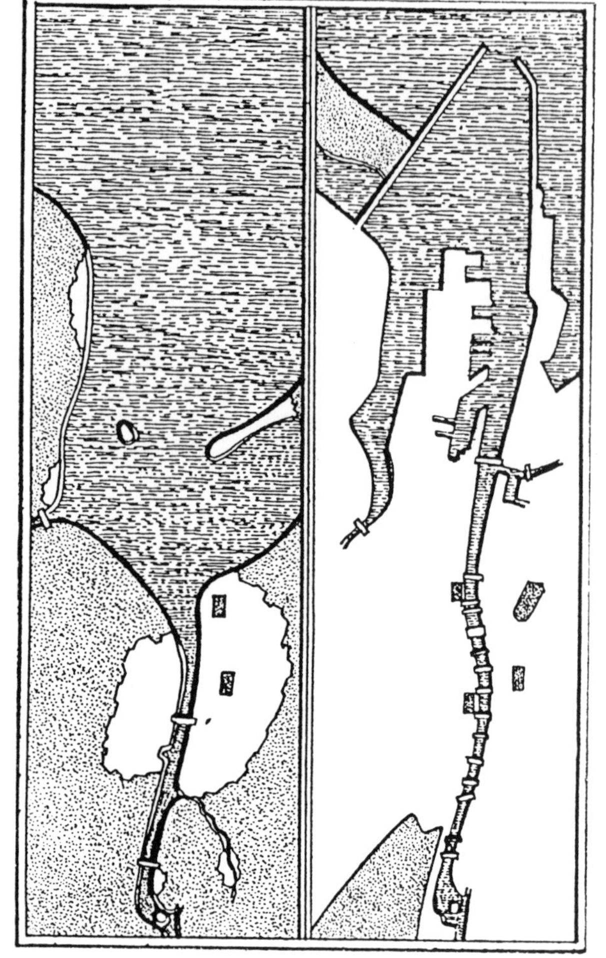

sheet of water was unbroken from Clontarf Road to Blackrock, a distance of about eight kilometres. Fairview Park did not exist and the shore followed the street known as Fairview Strand up to the estuary of the Tolka which itself was tidal for some distance above the site of Ballybough Bridge.

The shore line then followed along North Strand Road and Amiens Street until perhaps Talbot Street where it curved west to approach the present river bank near the mouth of the Bradogue at Ormonde Quay. Skirting the Four Courts, where there may at that time have been a low bluff, the line would have lain along Benburb Street and so under the slopes of Infirmary Road and Phoenix Park towards Chapelizod.

Crossing to the south bank, the high-tide shore line would have passed around a broad expanse of water at the confluence with the Camac. The tideway then narrowed again, following the north slope of the Thomas Street ridge and possibly inundating the present south quays and the land behind them as far downstream as the mouth of the Poddle. At Wood Quay in AD 800 the shore was more than a hundred metres south of the present river wall.

East of the mouth of the Poddle, the first sign of the estuary appeared. The shore line followed Fleet Street to Westmoreland Street, and then running east along Poolbeg Street swung off to the south along Sandwith Street. It continued then by Grand Canal Street along the verge of the marshes and sands of the Dodder near Lansdowne Road railway station. There it encountered the low but unyielding spit of Irishtown and Ringsend, and was forced to turn north to round the point of Ringsend, bending immediately south-east around the point and then following roughly Beach Road and Strand Road to the vicinity of Merrion Gates. From there to Blackrock it would have followed generally the edge of Rock Road. One remembers that the Dublin and Kingstown railway with its embankment at Booterstown was, in 800, still a thousand and thirty-four years in the future.

From 1600 onward, the high-tide shore line of the Liffey has been progressively contained within quay walls, land reclamations, and the great walls in the bay. Low tides no longer expose large areas of mud or sand within the region of the river channel. In the city, from the Pigeonhouse to Islandbridge, the width of the river is virtually the same at both extremes of the tide.

9. THE WEIR AND ISLANDS AT ISLANDBRIDGE

A short walk on the south side of the river, five minutes or so upstream of Sarah Bridge and past the sports field, leads out on to the south bank opposite the weir, one of the earliest man-made features of the river. To the left is a smooth expanse of water main-

tained at a constant level by the weir and lined with rowing clubs. Over the weir the river spills northward into a jumble of small channels between islands, and then almost at once turns east again to flow into the city. The high tide now reaches up to the weir, but rarely overtops it. This was not so in the thirteenth century. Then the river was an active thoroughfare, bringing town goods upstream and country produce down to the town, readily permitting the passage of fish and access for the boats of the fishermen.

In 1220 the citizens of Dublin complained to Henry III, saying "the prior and friars of the Hospital of Kilmainham have lately made a pool there whereby the city and citizens are much damnified." This would have been the weir in more or less its present position, and the purposes of the friars would have been to develop the millstream, which is still to be seen, and possibly also to reduce the contamination of the drinkable Liffey water by tidal salt water and city waste. The King sided with the citizens and ordered his justiciary to "cause to be surveyed by good and lawful men of the venue of Dublin the pool which the Hospitallers have made in the Avenesliz so that boats bearing wood and other necessaries to the vill of Dublin may pass and repass and fish may ascend and descend"; and he later ordered the obstruction to be removed. However, for reasons that remain unclear, this was never done.

The islands below the weirs are rarely mentioned. Modern maps show nine of them, ranging in size from small knobs of land four to five metres across up to the largest which is a hundred metres long and thirty metres wide. They most probably date back as natural features to before the time of the weir and may be the "Summer Ilands" mentioned early in the history of the city. They are covered with trees, undergrowth and rank grass, and give the appearance of having remained largely undisturbed by man all through their history.

There remains the riddle as to why the whole of this area of the river is known as Islandbridge. It may well be because of the ancient artificial island formed by the river and the millstream, or it may possibly arise from some association of a bridge with the natural islands. In this context, one cannot overlook the possibility that, in forming the weir, the friars merely converted one branch of the river into a millstream, rather than cut a new channel, and that the area on which the mills were built was already a natural island.

10. KILMEHANOC FORD

The Ford of Kilmehanoc, probably sited a little way upstream of the present Sarah Bridge, was one of the two principal fords of ancient Dublin. It and the Ath Cliath were both affected by the rise and fall of the tide, but Kilmehanoc, because of its location, would have been open for passage for longer periods than the more central Ath Cliath.

In AD 919, Niall Glundubh, High King of Ireland, was defeated by the Norsemen, and was himself killed, in an historic battle at the ford. Thereafter, the lordship of Dublin passed substantially to the Norsemen for over two hundred years.

Because of its strategic importance, the people of Dublin claimed the ford as part of the city. King John in his grant of AD 1200 to the citizens set the west boundary of the city at "the fords of Kilmehafach" and the river was regularly crossed at this place in the periodic ridings of the franchises of the city (see Note 71).

The remoteness of Kilmehanoc ford from the town proper tended to make it a preferred crossing for the lawless. It is said, for instance, that the O'Byrnes of Wicklow, using this route for a foray into Fingal in the early sixteenth century, came into conflict with a party of Dublin men who had mustered to block their passage. The encounter ended with defeat for the Dublin men at Sallcocks Wood which appears to have been at the north side of Phoenix Park near Cabra.

Bridges were built at various times on or near the ford (see Note 11), but it is of interest that as late as 1818, over twenty years after the construction of the present Sarah Bridge, the area of the ford was still known as Liffey Strand.

The ford has also been named Kilmaston, and the use and control of this crossing as a thoroughfare may be what is referred to in the ancient edict of the kings of Leinster: "that it is forbidden to ride a dirty black-heeled horse across the Magh Maistean." The Magh Maistean would have been the flattish land south of the river at this place, now lying between the river and Colbert and St John's Roads.

The fact that three different names have been given for this ford may suggest the difficulty of identifying particular locations. Eleven names can be quoted for this place. Several however are very much alike when spoken, and while the reference in John's grant to "fords" cannot be ignored, the precise position of this river crossing seems clear.

Even today, on looking at the river, it is not difficult to envisage a fordable crossing at this point; and, indeed, Oliver St John Gogarty in his famous swim may have experienced the shallowness of a ford, as it was in this vicinity that he climbed out of the Liffey following his escape from his kidnappers in January 1923.

11. KILMAINHAM AND SARAH BRIDGES

There have been at least three bridges at this place. The present bridge, Sarah Bridge, has a single elegant stone arch spanning thirty-one metres. It was named for Sarah, Countess of Westmoreland, who laid the foundation stone in 1791.

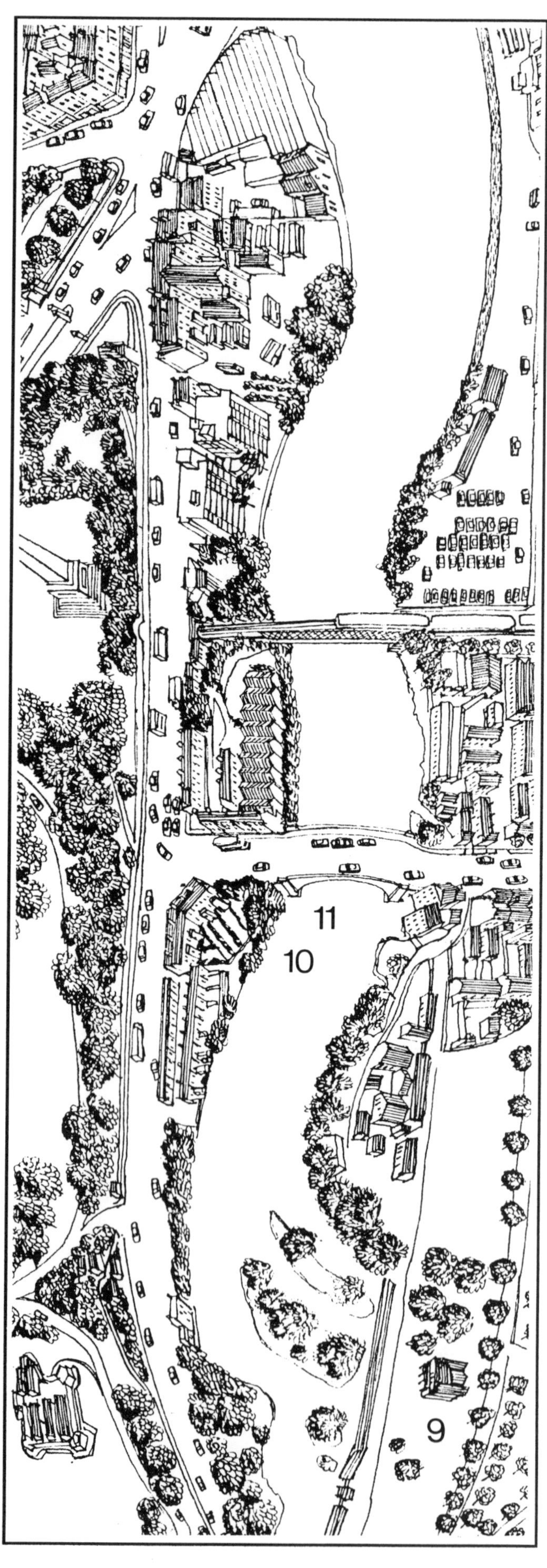

The need for this bridge arose from the dilapidation and partial collapse of the earlier Kilmainham Bridge. Built in 1578 on the orders of Sir Henry Sidney, lord deputy for Elizabeth I, and bearing, it is said, his coat of arms on its parapet, Kilmainham Bridge was some sixty metres upstream of the Sarah Bridge and close to the site of the ford of Kilmehanoc. It was a bridge of many spans and it stood for over two hundred years until 1788 when flooding caused part of it to collapse into the river where perhaps the coat of arms still lies.

Although Kilmainham Bridge was the second oldest road bridge across the Liffey in Dublin, it was not the oldest bridge on this particular site. Already in the thirteenth century, the mayor and citizens of Dublin had, after argument, extracted from the Prior of Kilmainham "free fishing in the waters of Avenelif from the bridge of Kilmaynan to the sea." This was surely a footbridge for crossing the ford at high tide and in times of flood, possibly suitable also for horse traffic. It would have been a narrow bridge, almost certainly of light timber construction; and for the next three hundred years it is likely that there was, for much of the time, a footbridge in this location.

There was certainly a bridge in 1535 when Sir William Skeffington, lord deputy for Henry VIII decided to cross the river there, while returning with a company of soldiers from Trim. The river was in flood, and the archers in the party, in making their way along the sodden north bank from the direction of Chapelizod, had been effectively disarmed through the loosening of their bowstrings and the feathers of their arrows by immersion in the water. As they approached the bridge, "a narrow structure", archers in the service of Silken Thomas Fitzgerald, who had risen in revolt against Henry the previous year, opened fire on them from a thicket on the south bank of the river. Skeffington however, who was known as "the gunner" because of his skill with firearms, dislodged the ambushing party by having his musketeers fire volleys of shot across the river, after which he and his men crossed and returned safely to the city.

12. THE ROYAL HOSPITAL AT KILMAINHAM

On the high, steeply-sided prow of land between the Liffey and the Camac, a monastery associated with the name of Saint Maigneann was built in the seventh century. It fell into decay during the Norse period in Dublin. During that time the strategically placed high ground was used as a base by Irish armies in some of their campaigns against the lords of Dublin, with Brian Boru spending some time there before the battle of Clontarf.

When the Normans subdued Dublin, perhaps partially to prevent the continued use of the site by potential enemies, Strongbow endowed the Knights Templars to establish a priory there in 1174. This was

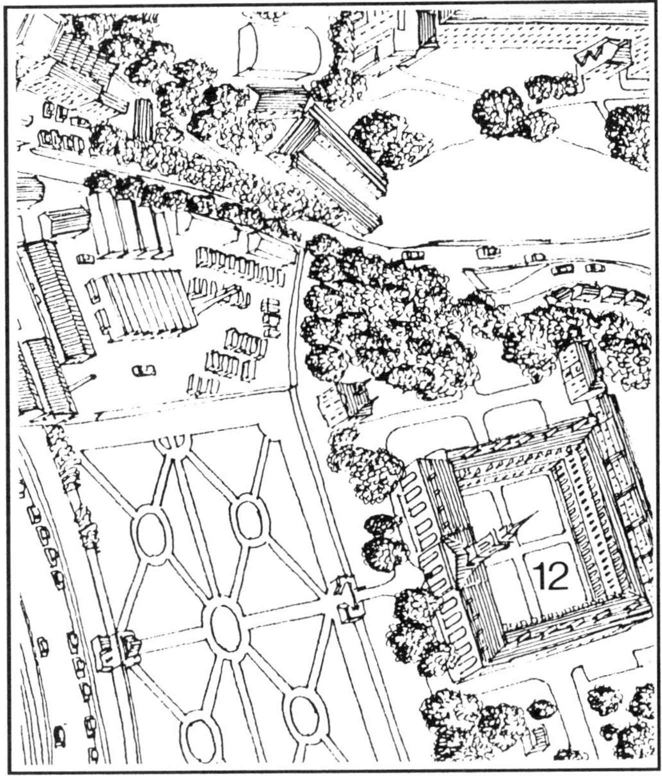

transferred to the Knights Hospitallers of Saint John of Jerusalem in 1312 and they remained there in community for a further 240 years.

Sir William Skeffington, lord deputy for King Henry VIII, and formulator of the "pardon of Maynooth", died in the priory in December 1535 at an age of over seventy years, worn out by illness and by his successful campaign against Silken Thomas Fitzgerald. Despite his ill health, he had been permitted, or required, to remain in office in October of that year, with Henry being prepared "to tolerate [his] sickness and debility."

In 1542, the priory was surrendered to Henry; and from 1559 until about 1620, when it was falling into decay, it served as a summer residence for the viceroys.

In 1677 the Duke of Ormonde, viceroy for King Charles II, proposed that a hospice for old and invalid soldiers be built on the site. In 1680 he laid the first foundation stone for the Royal Hospital, which was built to the design of William Robinson to accommodate three hundred residents. At that time the lands of Phoenix Park extended across the Liffey to include the priory site, but with the new foundation, Phoenix Park was reduced to include only lands on the north side of the river.

The Royal Hospital continued in its function until 1927, being shown in its prime by James Malton in his drawing of 1794. Its strategic importance continued to be appreciated. The commander-in-chief of the King's army in Ireland was accustomed to live there as Governor, contacts were kept as close as possible with the Royal Barracks across the river, and the hospital was used as a strong point by the British Army during the Easter Rising of 1916.

After a short period in the service of the Garda Siochána, the buildings of the hospital were used as storehouses until 1980, when a comprehensive programme of restoration, now largely completed, was begun.

13. LIFFEY VIADUCT

By the year 1860 Dublin had five railway termini, at Kingsbridge, Broadstone, Amiens Street, Westland Row and Harcourt Street. They all belonged to different railway companies and no two were connected, except by long cross-country links.

Seventeen years later, in 1877, the Great Southern and Western Railway with its main terminus at Kingsbridge (now Heuston) was encouraged to establish a rail link with the new cross-channel traffic facility being developed on the North Wall, between Guild Street and New Wapping Street.

Accordingly in that year, a railway bridge, the Liffey Viaduct, was built across the river downstream from Sarah Bridge; and a half-mile long tunnel, the longest railway tunnel in the city, was driven under

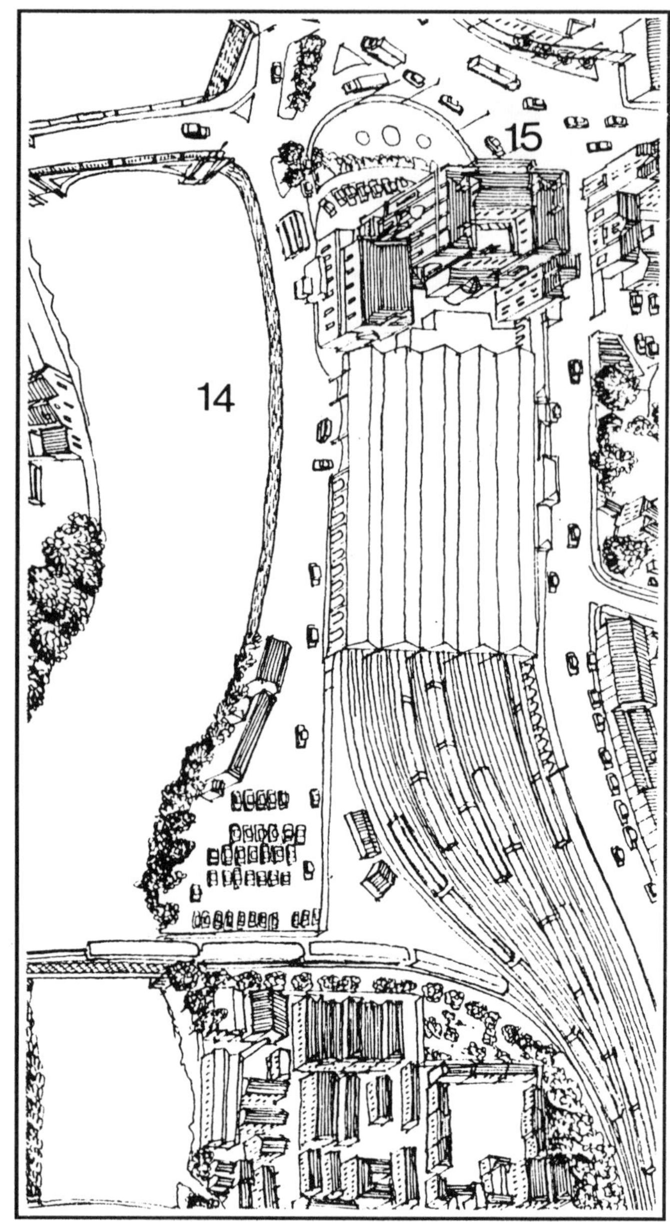

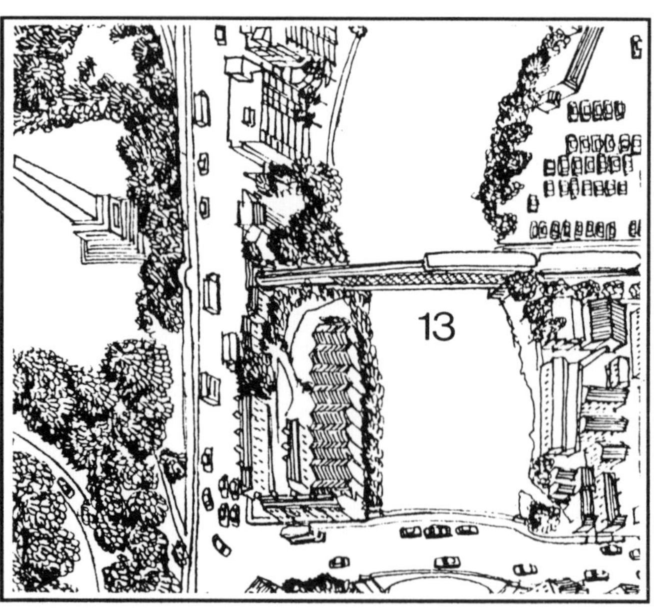

Conyngham Road and the Phoenix Park to carry the railway past Cabra, Glasnevin and Drumcondra to the North Wall.

The bridge consists of a metal lattice girder span over the river with three stone approach arches at each end. The entry of the line under the Phoenix Park can be identified by the stone arch built into the park wall on Conyngham Road.

14. THE RIVER CAMAC

The River Camac rises on Knockannavea Mountain near Brittas, and flows north through Slade, by Saggart, and across west County Dublin to Clondalkin. It then turns east and, passing quite close to the Grand Canal, near the waterworks built for Rathmines at Gallanstown in 1863, flows past Fox and Geese and Bluebell towards Drimnagh. Approaching the city, the river passes in a deep culvert below the Grand Canal and Davitt Road at Blackhorse Bridge, skirting Goldenbridge and passing under Emmet Road at Inchicore. Here it enters its final stretch flowing below Kilmainham Gaol, under the South Circular Road at the high-arched Kilmainham Bridge, and through the steeply-sided valley between the Royal Hospital and Old Kilmainham. Flowing under Bow Bridge, it goes underground on entering the lands at Dr Steevens Hospital, and emerges from under Heuston railway station at its point of discharge into the Liffey upstream of Heuston Bridge.

The Camac has always provided the motive power for mills for many purposes from Saggart to Kilmainham. In very early times, possibly even before the Norman conquest in the twelfth century, a millstream was drawn off from the river below Bow Bridge and taken across the Liffey Meadows to discharge into the Liffey near the Old Bridge (now Father Mathew Bridge). It may have been this millstream, which was covered by Guinness's brewery in the nineteenth century, that led to the formation and naming of Usher's Island.

Bow Bridge on the Camac is a very early river crossing. As such, it represented an important mark in the city boundaries and was regularly visited in the periodic riding of the franchises. In 1603 the mayor's party came riding "down the Murdring Lane [from Mount Brown to Bow Lane] to the water of Camocke and under the west arch of the bridge called Bowe bridge and tornid uppon the left hand under the high grownd of Kilmainehame to a deep forde ther where it was said the Annlyffe came of ould tyme ... and took boate ... and passed over the water of Cammocke."

Prior to the building of Heuston railway station, the confluence of the Camac and the Liffey was, at high tide, a broad expanse of water, as Lacy's eighteenth-century view of the Liffey from Phoenix Park suggests. This is supported by the details shown on the 1837 Ordnance Survey map of the area, and it becomes very clear why the mayoral party of 1603 would have needed to "take boate" to pass "over the water of Cammocke" in their tour of the city boundaries.

15. HEUSTON RAILWAY STATION

During the optimistic years of the early railway developments, the concept of providing the fastest possible mail service between London and America was always alive and under discussion. Charles Vignoles, following the success of the Dublin and Kingstown Railway in 1834, for which he was the engineer, was among those who were interested in the idea of a transatlantic port in the south-west of Ireland to be reached by train from London through Holyhead and Kingstown. To achieve this, a rail link was needed through Dublin. In 1836, Vignoles proposed the extension of the line from Westland Row to a terminus on the south bank of the Liffey near the present Rory O'More Bridge. This railway would have pierced through the houses in D'Olier Street and Westmoreland Street above first-floor level on its way to the quays, up which its supports would have strode, with one set in the river and the other in front of the quayside houses. This proposal was rejected and the link between Westland Row (Pearse) and the future Kingsbridge (Heuston) would not eventually be made until 1891.

In 1845, the Great Southern and Western Railway Company began construction of its railways; and in 1846 it built its Dublin terminus near the King's Bridge to a design by Sancton Wood. The terminus, with its attendant sheds, sidings, and marshalling yard, was built on the undeveloped meadows at the confluence of the Camac and the Liffey. It had as its immediate neighbour on the river bank upstream the earlier Royal Artillery barracks, later to become Clancy Barracks and the Ordnance Depot. The terminus was built over the channel of the Camac, burying it in the culvert in which it now flows under the station into the Liffey. The terminus buildings were extended in 1911, the architect being J C Dewhurst. The name of the station was later changed from Kingsbridge to Heuston in commemoration of Captain Seán Heuston, whose name was also given to the nearby King's Bridge.

16. THE QUAYS IN GENERAL

The Liffey quays, which are listed in two subsequent notes, were almost all built in stone. In their early days, the waterside edge of most of them was unprotected, which is indeed the most natural condition for a quay; or there were houses or high walls along the river, with access to the water being by slips between or through them. The stone parapets on the

Liffey quays were built generally at the end of the eighteenth and early in the nineteenth century, mostly under the direction of George Halpin Senior, inspector and later engineer for the Port Corporation. Extensive lengths of the quays downstream still have unprotected edges. Under state legislation, the maintenance of the quay walls from Rory O'More Bridge to the sea, being technically in navigable waters, is the responsibility of the Dublin Port and Docks Board, while the quay walls further upstream are under the control of Dublin Corporation.

Sea-going river traffic has been steadily pushed downstream over the last three hundred years by the successive building of river bridges eastwards, and there is now no sea-going traffic west of Talbot Memorial Bridge. The last quay up-river to be in active use was Victoria Quay where the Guinness steam barges with their distinctive folding funnels continued to operate until 1961. The openings in the parapets which gave access to their jetties can still be identified by the newness of the stonework used to fill them.

17. THE SOUTH QUAYS

The quays on the south bank of the Liffey today, listed in the order of their construction, are as follows. The year given for each is not precise, as the building of a quay was rarely the work of a single year. Other names sometimes used for the quays are given in parentheses.

Wood Quay	900	(Coal Quay)
Merchants Quay	1300	(Bridge Street Quay and, jointly with Wood Quay, Dublin Quay)
Blind Quay	early seventeenth century	
Old Custom House Quay	1620	
Usher's Quay	1650	
Usher's Island	1650	
Essex Quay	1680	
Aston Quay	1700	(i: Aston Quay which now extends from O'Connell Bridge to the Ha'penny Bridge, formerly finished at Bedford Row; and the quay from there to the Ha'penny Bridge was called Crampton Quay, *c*1760. ii: Aston Quay would appear to have included Hawkins Quay)

Saint George's Quay	1700	(generally known as George's, or George, Quay: and would appear to have included White's Quay)
City Quay	1700	
Sir John Rogerson's Quay	1720	
Burgh Quay	1800	
Wellington Quay	1820	
Victoria Quay	1850	
South Quay	1960	(South Bank Quay: downstream of Ringsend)

In addition to these built quays, three names appear in Lazers Hill around 1700. These are:
Brookes Quays;
Crosses Quay;
Nichols or Nicholas' Quay.

These would appear to have been private mooring slips and went out of action when Sir John Rogerson's Quay was made.

The "harbours" at the mouth of the Poddle and the Stein have not been mentioned, not being quays.

18. THE NORTH QUAYS

The quays on the north bank of the Liffey today, listed in their order of construction, are as follows. The same comments apply as for the south bank quays.

Inns Quay	1250	(developed in 1700; Kings Inns Quay)
Ormond Quay Lower	1700	(Jervis' Quay)
Ormond Quay Upper	1700	
Arran Quay	1700	
Bachelors Walk	1700	(this quay included part of Eden Quay at one time)
North Wall Quay	1750	(North Quay)
Ellis Quay	1800	(the east part was built in about 1760 and called Back Quay)
Eden Quay	1800	(included the earlier Iron Quay)
Custom House	1800	
Custom House Quay	1820	
Sarsfield Quay	1830	(built as Pembroke Quay, which included the earlier Sand Quay)
Wolfe Tone Quay	1850	(Albert Quay)
North Quay Extension	1890	(North Wall Extension)
Alexandra Quay	1935	
Alexandra Quay East	1955	

Two names also seen are East Quay which was sometimes used for the East Wall, and North Strand Quay, an unfinished stretch that was later substantially taken in by Eden Quay.

Saint Mary's Abbey Quay which was in service for about five hundred years from 1000 is not mentioned, as it does not exist today.

19. SEAN HEUSTON BRIDGE

Following the construction of the Royal Barracks in the first decade of the eighteenth century and Dr Steevens Hospital in 1713, the need for a bridge across the Liffey to replace the ferry granted to Dr Steevens, was a matter frequently raised. A visit to Dublin by King George IV in 1821 led to an opportunity to use funds publicly subscribed to build a bridge, to be called King's Bridge in commemoration of the royal visit. Several designs were prepared and it is said that it was the King himself who decided on which to adopt. This was a single-span seven-ribbed cast iron arched bridge to a design by George Papworth. It was an early example of cast iron bridge construction and possibly the earliest major road bridge made with that material in Ireland. The foundation stone was laid in December 1827 by the lord lieutenant, Marquis Wellesley. The castings were made in the Phoenix Iron Works which were located close by and the bridge was completed in 1828.

The bridge, which bears the date of the royal visit, 1821, was re-named Sarsfield Bridge in 1922 and Seán Heuston Bridge some years later. It carries the following inscription:

Sé ainm an droichid seo anois ná
DROICHEAD SEAN HEUSTON
i gcuimhne
Capt Seán Heuston
(Fianna Eireann)
a thug a anam ar gon phoblacht na h-Eireann
8 Bealtaine 1916
Ar dheasláimh Dé go raibh a anam
Cumann na nUigeann Náisiúnta a thóg 1955

20. FRANK SHERWIN BRIDGE

As part of the reorganisation of the flow of traffic along the Liffey quays, it was decided to build a major road bridge across the river immediately downstream of Seán Heuston Bridge. A three-span reinforced concrete bridge was designed by Richard Fowler of Dublin Corporation and built by the company of Irishenco Limited. It opened to traffic in 1979.

The new bridge was named for Frank Sherwin, who had died shortly before, to commemorate his life's work for the city as a member of Dublin Corporation and Dáil Eireann.

A plaque on the bridge carries the following inscription in Irish and in English:

THIS BRIDGE WAS OPENED OFFICIALLY BY THE RIGHT HONOURABLE, THE LORD MAYOR, COUNCILLOR DAN BROWNE: 28 AUGUST, 1982.

A second plaque is inscribed as follows:

IRISH CONCRETE SOCIETY AWARD 1982: IRISHENCO LTD. DUBLIN.

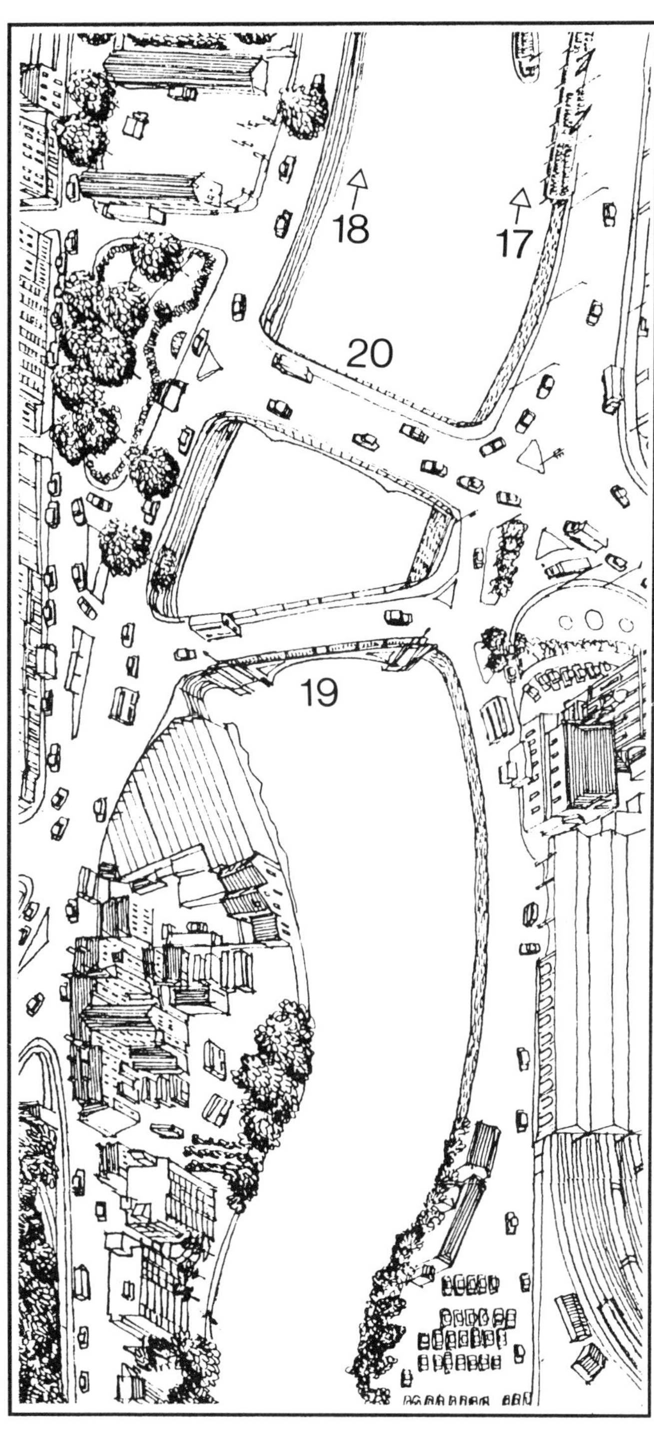

21. COLLINS BARRACKS

In 1700, at the end of a century of war and tur-
bulence, and at the beginning of another which would
know no rebellion until it was ninety-eight years old,
King William gave orders to build in Dublin the
largest military barracks in his dominions.

In 1701 the foundations were laid for the Royal
Barracks, to be built to a design by Thomas Burgh,
the Surveyor-General. The work was finished in the
reign of Queen Anne about four years later. The barracks could accommodate four regiments of foot and
four of horse, perhaps 3000-4000 men. It was the principal barracks in Dublin, and all formal guard and
escort duties at the Castle and in the city were
mounted from there.

The barracks, probably shown in its original form
by Rocque in 1756, was subsequently enlarged to
occupy, with its outbuildings and parade grounds, a
rectangular area 330 metres long and 150 metres
broad. Some idea of its great extent may be gained
from Malton's drawing of 1796, and George Petrie's
drawing of the King's Bridge in 1829.

The Royal Barracks was re-named Collins Barracks to commemorate General Michael Collins
(1890-1922) the first commander-in-chief of the
National Army of the Free State of Ireland.

22. SOYER'S FOOD KITCHEN

There is a riverside area that seems never to have
been built on, a little way upstream of Rory O'More
Bridge, between Benburb Street (once known as Barrack Street) and the present site of Wolfe Tone Quay.

In the winter of 1847, while the great famine was
raging in Ireland, there were many in Dublin who
were short of food to the point of starvation. To offer
assistance, the government invited Alexis Soyer,
"perhaps the most famous chef in Europe" in the
words of Cecil Woodham-Smith, to help them. He had
concocted a soup of such nourishment that one bowl-
ful eaten with some bread would sustain a man for a
day, and he was asked to provide this meal in Dublin.
Woodham-Smith records in *The Great Hunger* that
"Soyer's new model soup kitchen was constructed in
front of the Royal Barracks in Dublin and opened on
April 5 [1847]. It was a wooden building about forty
feet long and thirty feet wide with a door at each end;
in the centre was a three-hundred gallon soup boiler;
a hundred bowls, to which spoons were attached by
chains, were let into long tables. The people assembled outside the building and were first admitted to a
narrow passage, a hundred at a time; a bell rang; they
were let in, drank their soup, received a portion of
bread, and left by the other door. The bowls were
rinsed, the bell rang again and another hundred were
admitted."

One must be grateful to Soyer for his compassion

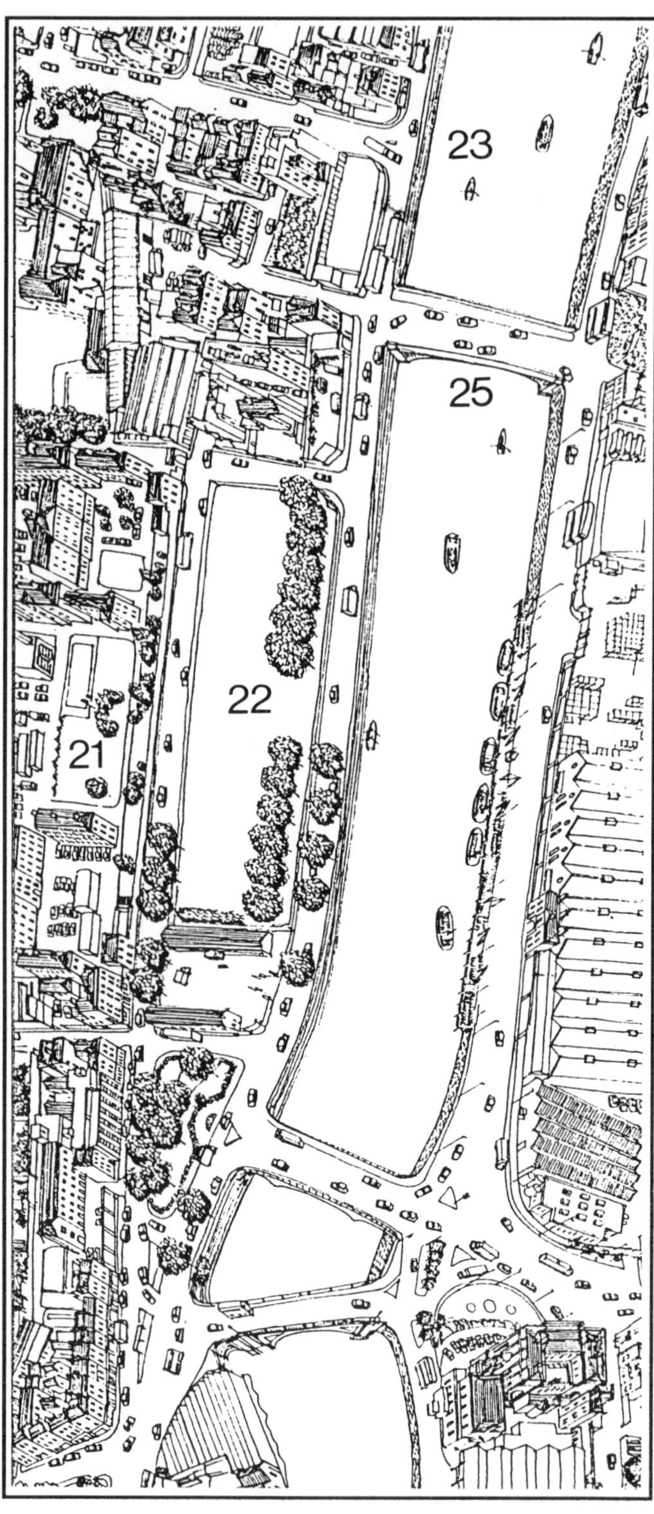

but it was felt by some that the sensitivity of this exercise did not altogether match its efficiency. Colonel John Fox Burgoyne, an army engineer and chairman of the Board of Public Works in Ireland, wrote of the operation that "it was a mistake to feed the destitute like wild animals."

23. GRAVEL WALK SLIP AND SLIPS IN GENERAL

Slips have the merit that they can be used to reach the water's edge at any stage of the tide. There were many such slips along the banks of the Liffey and there are numerous references in the records to their construction, ownership, and maintenance. One often mentioned was the Bagnio Slip beside which one of the city ferries had a landing place. Another was the Fysshe Slypp near Fyan's Castle.

The Gravel Walk Slip, situated on the north bank of the river downstream of Rory O'More Bridge and occupying nearly half of the river frontage between John Street and Ellis Street, formerly called Silver Street, had some unique aspects. It formed a bay in the river some fifty metres wide and sixty metres deep, south to north, and Rocque's map of 1756 permits one to believe that its north shore may possibly have been the primeval shingly or muddy shore line of the river tideway. There was very little building around the bay, and the Gravel Walk, an extension of Barrack Street, passed along its northern edge. The proximity of the Smithfield market, the Royal Barracks, and five recorded timber yards points to the bay and slip as a likely dock for handling small commercial river lighters as well as timber from ships in the estuary, floated up the river as logs or roughly-made rafts.

The general neighbourhood, lying as it did between the Barracks and the markets, could at times be turbulent, as Kipling's poem "Belts", written in 1890, tells:

*There was a row in Silver Street, that's near to Dublin
    quay*
Between an Irish regiment an' English cavalree;
It started at Revelly and it lasted on till dark.
*The first man dropped at Harrison's, the last forninst
    the Park.*

It was a good-natured affair at first with the *"Polis"* being thrown into the Liffey because *"The English were too drunk to know and the Irish didn't care."*

Tragedy struck when a side-arm was drawn and a man was killed. *"An' so we all were murderers that started out in fun."*

The narrator, speaking from his prison cell, finishes on a philosophical note:

'Tis all a merricle to me as in the clink I lie;
There was a row in Silver Street — begod,
    I wonder why.

The Gravel Walk Slip was filled-in early in the nineteenth century and Ellis Quay is shown in 1837 as continuous from Mellowes Bridge to Rory O'More Bridge.

24. THE RIVER FERRIES

Where there are people who wish to cross a river and goods to be carried, but there are no bridges, ferries will flourish. It is possible that from Norse times onwards, and perhaps earlier, there were ferries plying for trade across the Liffey. The first recorded ferry would appear to have been in 1386 when, following the collapse of part of the Old Bridge, King Richard II, to aid in the repair of the bridge and to overcome the inconvenience caused by its collapse, granted the mayor, bailiffs and citizens (for four years) the city ferry over the Liffey, with permission to take a toll of a farthing from every man and woman carried.

The City Assembly must later have assumed the right to grant licences to operate ferries because in 1634, during the reign of Charles I, they come into conflict with his lord deputy about this right.

On 14 March 1665, King Charles II, then being in the seventeenth year of his reign and wishing to thank his people of Dublin for their loyalty to him during the Cromwell intervention, made a grant "to the Maior, Sheriffes, Commons, and cittizens of the said citty of Dublin and their successors of the ferry-boat over the River Anna Liffie." The fare was not to exceed a halfpenny and he required them "from sun-rising and an hour before and until sun-setting and an hour after to give due attendance...with sufficient boats and other things necessary."

Arguments soon broke out between entrepreneurs who wished to profit as ferry lessees. In 1669 Nathaniel Fowkes, the legal lessee at the time, was complaining that "his boats are dayly stopt and interrupted by Mr Mabbott and others." Ferries were established where there were no bridges, and according as bridges were built, the ferry crossings were moved to new locations, generally downstream of the bridge at any time nearest the sea. Thus in 1729, the Essex Bridge (now Grattan Bridge) having been built, an attempt was made to amalgamate all ferries into a single operation from Dirty Lane down to Ringsend Point. Dirty Lane, which then extended to the river as a slip, is now Temple Lane, and terminates in Temple Bar.

In 1756 John Rocque in his map showed ferries at Dirty Lane (by then called Temple Lane), Porter's Row (now Bedford Row) and just upstream of Hawkins Street (the "Old Ferry"). Other stations mentioned at that time were at the Bagnio Slip, and at a crossing from Fleet Alley (now Westmoreland Street) to Bachelors Lane (the present O'Connell Street not then extending to the river). The Fleet Alley approach to the south bank was far from salubrious. It is said that the ground between College Green and the river "was occupied with lime kilns, and lanes and alleys of the most wretched description," the principal passage being Fleet Alley.

It is probable that, whether under lease or not, there would have been a ferry plying from Ringsend to the end of the North Wall all during this period. At the other end of the city, a ferry granted to the trustees of Dr Steevens Hospital in 1720, near the site of one of the city gallows in Parkgate Street, remained in service until the opening of the King's Bridge in 1828. In 1778, shortly after the development of the Circular Road, an application was made for a ferry at the Marine School on Sir John Rogerson's Quay, to accommodate traffic using that road. The north bank station would have been at Guild Street, and it is of interest to realise that the trustees of the Circular Road must have seen Portland Row, Seville Place, and Guild Street as the extension of the road to the north bank of the river. This was to be a general ferry. A horse fare was probably one penny and the ferry would have been expected to carry cattle, merchandise and carriages, as well as people.

During the eighteenth century, as well as the cross-river ferries, there was a ferry that plied up and down the river from Ringsend to George's Quay, bringing passengers to and from the cross-channel vessels that sailed into Ringsend and to anchorages further down the South Wall. Hammond has recorded that Jonathan Swift, George Frederick Handel, John Wesley, and Peg Woffington were among those who came to Dublin in this way between 1723 and 1747.

In 1815 permission was given to replace the Bagnio Slip ferry with a permanent toll footbridge, the Liffey Bridge or Ha'penny Bridge, and this was opened in 1816 with the proviso that the toll should not exceed one halfpenny per person. This new departure and the building of Carlisle (later O'Connell) Bridge in 1794 effectively wiped out the ferries in the city. From then until 1984 the ferry traffic was confined to the reach of the river between the new Custom House and Ringsend. The need for transporting cross-channel passengers into the city by river was also, for various reasons, disappearing.

Business on the lower river was brisk and not always prudent. In 1871 a complaint was lodged that the ferry boat could be "dangerously overcrowded often with more than thirty people on dark winter nights," and there were reports of passengers falling into the river due to inadequate lighting at the landing places.

In 1881 there were five ferry routes on the lower Liffey. These were described as follows:

	Station at South Side	*Station at North Side*
1	At No. 14 City Quay (between Moss Street and Princes Street)	Transit shed at east side of Custom House Dock
2	Creighton Street	Commons Street
3	At No 29 Rogerson's Quay (beside Lime Street and Cardiff Lane)	At west side of Royal Canal
4	At Messrs Kurtz, Coal Tar Distillers (between Forbes Street and Benson Street)	Near Wapping Street
5	East Point of the South Wall (Sir John Rogerson's Quay) and Great Britain Quay, on the Dodder	At Messrs Martin's saw mills on the north side of the river

This last-named sometimes plied to Ringsend Point instead.

On 21 October 1984 the Eastlink Bridge was opened to traffic. On the previous day the last formal ferry crossing of the river was made. The fare was now ten pence per person carried. It was on the fifth route described above and it marked the end of the recorded era of ferry service in Dublin, extending over at least six hundred years.

25. RORY O'MORE BRIDGE

Also known as Bloody, Barrack, Victoria, Victoria and Albert, Watling Street, Emancipation, and Saint James or James's Bridge.

The first bridge on this site, a wooden structure, was built in 1670. This made it the second oldest bridge in the city proper, and its erection angered those who had a vested interest in the ferry service nearby, as well as those who felt it to be "against the general sense of this citty." Incited by some means, a number of apprentices gathered at the bridge to pull it down. They were however seized and were being taken to the Bridewell gaol when a rescue attempt was made. In the ensuing skirmish, four were killed. It was this incident that gave the bridge the name of Bloody Bridge which has stuck to it ever since.

The life of a wooden bridge is rarely long and in about 1704 a new bridge in stone with four arches was built on the site.

About 150 years later, Gilbert noted in his history that this bridge had been closed to traffic, and in 1857 a contract was awarded to John Killeen of Malahide to build another crossing on the site. At this time, the Corporation for Preserving and Improving the Port of Dublin, successor to the Ballast Office, was responsible for the whole of the Liffey from the sea up to and including Bloody Bridge (except for the Liffey Bridge, or Ha'penny Bridge), and they decided that the new structure was to be a "metropolitan bridge over a river there navigable by laden barges." A handsome single-arched span of iron was supplied by Robert Daglish Junior, Saint Helens Foundry, Lancashire, in 1858, and at the end of a prolonged and difficult contract, the new bridge was opened by Queen Victoria in 1863.

In 1929, the centenary of Catholic emancipation was commemorated in Ireland by a High Mass in the Phoenix Park attended by roughly half-a-million people, followed by Benediction at the bridge. An inscription on the east parapet reads as follows :

1829-1929
ANNO CENTESIMO POST IVRA POLITICA
MAIORIBUS NOSTRIS CATHOLICIS REDDITA
IX KAL IVL MCMXXIX
EDVARDVS ARCHIEP DVBLINEN
EX ALTARE SVPER HVNC PONTEM APTE
STRVCTO
BENEDIXIT CVM SSMO SACRAMENTO
MVLTITVDINEM QVINGENORVM FERE MILIVM
FIDELIVM
ADSTANTE NVNTIO S SEDIS SPECIALI
VNA CVM HIBERNORVM ANTISTIBVS
VNIVERSIS

This may be translated as:

"1829-1929 : On 23 June 1929, the centennial anniversary year of the restoration of political rights to our Catholic forefathers, Edward, Archbishop of Dublin, imparted Blessing of the Most Holy Sacrament from an altar fittingly constructed on this bridge to a vast congregation of the Faithful, numbering almost five hundred thousand, and in the presence of a special representative of the Holy See, accompanied by all the bishops of Ireland."

For some time afterwards, the bridge was known as Emancipation Bridge. It had been renamed Rory O'More Bridge in 1922, but that name cannot have been in general use in 1929. Rory O'More, of Laois, was a leading figure in the rising of 1641, and a general officer in the Army of the Confederation of Kilkenny. On one occasion he escaped from pursuers by boat, being taken up-river past this bridge site to rescuers waiting at Islandbridge. An ancestor, also Rory O'More, of Dunamase, was a sixteenth-century leader of the Irish against Elizabeth I.

26. RICHMOND GUARD TOWER

Until the early nineteenth century, the quays on the south bank of the Liffey ended upstream with Usher's Island and Rory O' More Bridge at the foot of Watling Street. At that time, while much of the area now occupied by Guinness's brewery still consisted of tree-lined fields, a new avenue, described as a military road, was opened to link the Royal Hospital in Kilmainham to the end of the quays.

Whether for some perceived need of protection or privacy, or through a sense of splendour, a stone gate tower designed by the architect Francis Johnston was built in 1812 to terminate the view along the quay and to control access to the new road. This tower, the Richmond Guard Tower, proved an obstacle to traffic when, in 1846, the Great Southern and Western Railway Company built its terminus at Kingsbridge. In 1847 the tower was taken down at the expense of the railway company and re-erected on the South Circular Road at the west entrance to the Royal Hospital where it can be seen today. A drawing made by George Petrie in 1819 shows the tower in its original location beside the Rory O'More Bridge as it then was, and also offers a delightful contemporary impression of that part of the Liffey.

27. MOIRA HOUSE

The Rawdon family was granted the baronetcy of Moira, in County Down, in 1665 by King Charles II; in 1762 Sir John Rawdon (1720-1793) was created first Earl of Moira. In 1752, he built Moira House on Usher's Island, which was then a highly fashionable quarter of the city. It was an elegant three-storied house and became known in Dublin for its hospitality. The names of John Wesley, Charles James Fox, Henry Grattan, Theobald Wolfe Tone and Thomas Russell, "the man from God-knows-where", are recorded among the countless guests received. The Dowager Countess of Moira befriended Lord Edward Fitzgerald and his family, and his wife Pamela was staying at Moira house when told of Lord Edward's arrest by Major Sirr on 19 May 1798.

After the death of the Dowager Countess early in the nineteenth century, the house fell into disrepair and in 1820 was described as being "many years in a ruinous state uninhabited."

In 1826 the Association for the Suppression of Mendicancy in Dublin, which had started its work in Hawkins Street in 1818, took over Moira House as a Mendicity Institute. The top storey was removed and the two remaining storeys extended in plan. The elegance was lost, but the tradition of hospitality lived on. It is recorded that in 1899 over 55,000 people were helped by its services. The building was demolished about twenty-five years ago. The site is now occupied by a day centre of the Eastern Health Board, the front boundary wall and railings of the Mendicity Institution being retained. The Mendicity Institution itself has been re-located on Island Street, which runs parallel to Usher's Island Quay.

The Mendicity Institution was occupied for two days during the Easter Rising of 1916 by Seán

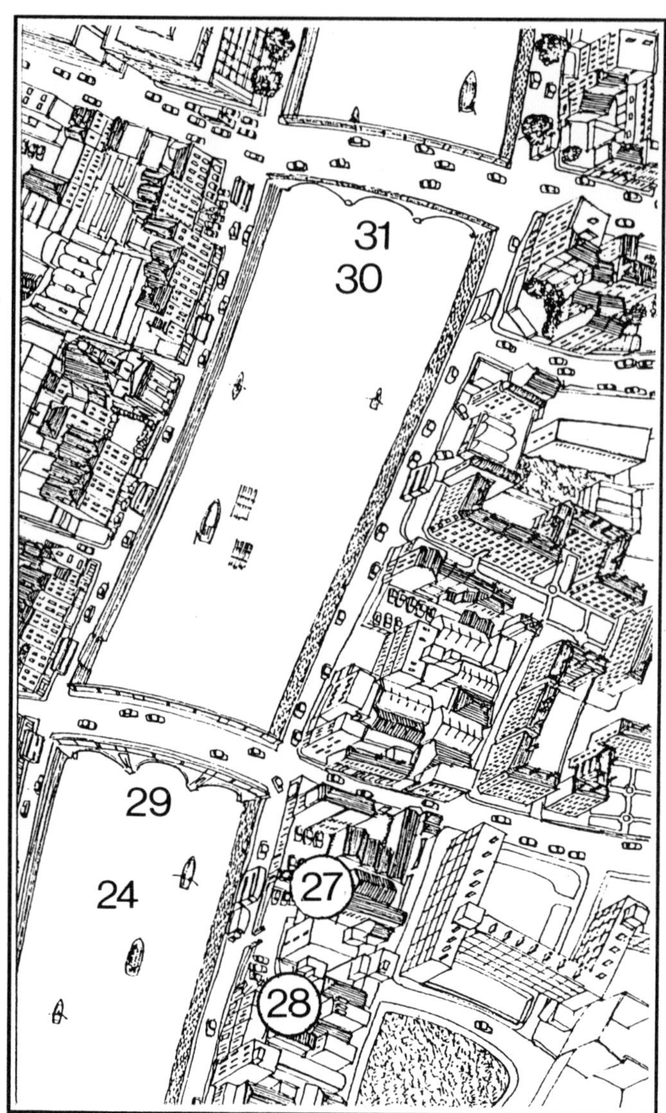

Heuston and twenty men as an outpost from the Four Courts.

Usher's Island is no longer as fashionable a quarter as formerly, and Moira House has been justly included by Frederick O'Dwyer as an example of "lost Dublin" in his book of that name.

28. USHER'S ISLAND

The name Usher's Island today refers mainly to the short length of the south bank quay on the Liffey between Mellowes Bridge and Rory O'More Bridge.

The Usher family has been well known in Dublin since Arnold Usher was mayor of the city in 1467, and their principal residence was on the bank of the Liffey in Bridge Street just west of the Old Bridge (now Father Mathew Bridge). There had been a fortified house in this location, which lay at the north-west corner of the city walls from as early as 1300.

The millstream from the River Camac had one of its channels of discharge into the Liffey beside this house at a confluence that later came to be known as Usher's Pill, and another through a branch mill-stream entering the Liffey at Bloody Bridge. The area, roughly rectangular in plan, between the Liffey, the main millstream and the two discharge streams was probably what was known as Usher's Island at the time. It is not clear whether Usher's house was or was not on Usher's Island as the maps differ. Easy access would have been available over a private bridge as Usher's Pill cannot have been wide. By 1728, when Brooking's map was published, it had gone underground.

At first, the Liffey bank at Usher's Island was a "strand" and would have been a place for beaching boats at low tide. During the seventeenth and early eighteenth centuries, the Ushers developed the island. Two formal quays, Usher's Quay and Usher's Island, were built, and a series of six slips was made. However, because of the Old Bridge, these facilities would have been of little use to seagoing sailing ships.

During the fifteenth century, the Dominican friars of Saint Saviour's on the north bank had a school of philosophy and divinity on Usher's Island. This property was transferred to the Ushers in the sixteenth century. In later times, the island, as well as being a fashionable place to live, was a centre for commerce and industry. Rocque shows a large timber yard there in 1756, and a distillery and a pottery have also been recorded.

The area lying to the south of Usher's Island, up the hill towards Bonham Street, was not developed until the end of the eighteenth century. Before then it may have been used as a rubbish dump. The fact that the roadway along the south boundary of the island had its name changed from Dunghill Lane in 1756 to Island Street in 1837 supports this suggestion.

29. MELLOWES BRIDGE

This bridge has also been known as Arran, Arons, Queen's, Bridewell, Ellis's, and Queen Maev.

In a slightly headstrong period of Dublin bridge building from 1670 to 1684, four new bridges were made along a one-kilometre stretch of the Liffey. One of these was Arran Bridge, named for the Earl of Arran, and built in 1684.

The collapse of this bridge in 1763 is described by George Semple: "A rapid land-flood broke the moorings of a raft of timber at the Barrack-slip, and carried it down to Queen's [*sic*] Bridge, where it unluckily lodged quite across the middle arch. The piers of this bridge were built on the surface of the bed of the river, as most of the former bridges were. This raft of timber, obstructing the current of the surface, in like manner increased the power of it at the bottom and within the space of a few hours totally demolished the bridge."

The bridge was rebuilt as Queen's Bridge in 1768 under the direction of Charles Vallancey, antiquary and soldier, with the army rank of Engineer-in-Ordinary in Ireland. His bridge, which is the one we see today, is the oldest surviving bridge across the Liffey, and is held by many to be the most elegant in the city.

The name of the bridge was changed to Queen Maev in 1922, and in 1942 the name of Mellowes Bridge was given to it. A plaque on the bridge in Irish and English reads as follows:

MELLOWS [*sic*] BRIDGE,
TO HONOUR THE MEMORY OF
LIEUT GENERAL LIAM MELLOWS [*sic*]
IRISH REPUBLICAN ARMY.
WHO GAVE HIS LIFE FOR THE REPUBLIC OF
IRELAND.
8th DECEMBER 1922

GO NDEINIDH DIA TRÓCAIRE AR ANAMNAIBH
ÁR MARTAR UILE
ERECTED BY THE NATIONAL GRAVES
ASSOCIATION
1942

The bridge is named as Mellowes Bridge on the current Ordnance Survey map.

30. ATH CLIATH

It is reasonable that the first crossing of the river at Dublin would have been a ford, and Ath Cliath, the ford of the hurdles, has been mentioned in Irish history for nearly two thousand years. The fact that the river was tidal at the crossing place makes it clear that the ford was unusable for much of the time, and also raises the question of whether the walking surfaces extending across the tideway were stabilised in any way, and if so, how this was done.

Clarke's map locates Ath Cliath about ninety metres upstream of Father Mathew Bridge. He shows it passing through Usher's Pill and connecting the line of Bow Street on the north bank to that of Saint Augustine Street on the south bank, this being the suggested route of the Slige Midluachra, one of the early great roads of Ireland.

At an early date in the history of Dublin (Baile Atha Cliath in Irish), this ford was supplemented by a bridge, which, after several transmutations, has become the present Father Mathew Bridge.

31. FATHER MATHEW BRIDGE

Also known as *King John's, Dublin, Friars, Old, Church Street,* and *Whitworth.*

It seems clear that, perhaps by the year 1000, there was a bridge across the Liffey near Ath Cliath, compensating for the ford's frequent tidal closures. Its name appears as Danes Bridge, Ostmans Bridge and the crossing features as Droichet Dubhghaill in the closing stages of the battle of Clontarf in 1014. Whether it was stone, or timber, or timber on sophisticated stone foundations is not known.

In 1214, King John granted the citizens of Dublin "that they [may] make a bridge over the Anna Liffey whenever they may deem most convenient for the use of the city; and that they may, if advisable, cause the bridge previously constructed to be destroyed." The bridge was built, most probably of stone, and on the site of the present Father Mathew bridge, and it was finished by about 1230. From the beginning, Ostmans Gate, a fortified house, stood at the south end of the bridge, leading to the ancient thoroughfare of Bridge Street. By 1307 there were shops and possibly other buildings on the bridge itself.

It was from this bridge, or more likely the earlier one, that the famous bow shot of Little John was reputedly loosed. Little John, a companion of Robin Hood, is said to have fled to Ireland after the capture of his friend, and, while in Dublin, to have been invited to demonstrate his strength as an archer. The story tells that he took his stance on the bridge and shot an arrow a prodigious distance into Oxmantown where it lodged in an earth mound that became known as "Little John his Shot".

King John's bridge collapsed in 1385 and was replaced in 1428 with a stone bridge of four arches, a bridge that would last for nearly 400 years and would come to be known simply as The Bridge and later, not surprisingly, as the Old Bridge. There is no record of extensive building on the Old Bridge, but there was a chapel of "Saint Mary on the Bridge" at the north end for over a hundred years in the fifteenth and sixteenth centuries.

The history associated with the Bridge of Dublin needs more telling than can be fitted in these notes.

Located at the north-west corner of the walled city, and being the only Liffey bridge in Dublin for more than 450 years, it figured largely in the life of the city. Thus Queen Elizabeth I favoured it with a public clock in 1573, and again with her Royal Arms. In 1603, two of its arches were declared to be "ruynated and decaied". In 1640, Charles I fined the city 200 pounds for not attending to its repair. In 1652, the head of Sir Phelim O'Neill, executed for his part in the Confederation of Kilkenny, was set upon the Ostmans Gate. In 1666, the city was seeking a "knowing artist" to erect a sundial on the bridge. In 1706 the Ostmans Gate, being in ruins, was finally pulled down and the bridge made open. In 1764, it was lit for the first time, with four lamps; and in 1776, the Wide Streets Commissioners were engaged in removing the labyrinth of old houses that clustered around its north end and had turned the passage from Inns Quay to Arran Quay into a medieval adventure.

In 1806 John Carr, a visitor, found the Old Bridge to be a "crazy dirty wretched pile of antiquity". He could truthfully have added that it was bolstered up with timber and held together with iron. By 1813 it was described as tottering and steps were being taken to prevent its use by vehicles; in 1815 it was decided that the time had come to rebuild. George Knowles, already engaged in the construction of O'Donovan Rossa Bridge, offered to build a virtually identical bridge on the Old Bridge site, again therefore to the design of James Savage, and for about the same cost. The foundation stone was laid by the lord lieutenant, the Earl of Whitworth, in October 1816, and the bridge which was named for him was opened to traffic in 1818. It is of interest to note that, had Whitworth declined to give his name to the new bridge, the approved substitute was to have been Waterloo Bridge.

The Whitworth Bridge, the third bridge on this site in 750 years, continues in service today. It was renamed Dublin Bridge in 1922. It is now named the Father Mathew Bridge, and an inscription in Irish and English reads as follows.

FATHER MATHEW BRIDGE
+
THIS BRIDGE HAS BEEN RENAMED TO
COMMEMORATE
THE INAUGURATION 100 YEARS AGO OF THE
APOSTOLATE OF TEMPERANCE BY FATHER
THEOBALD
MATHEW O.M. CAP.
1838 + 1938

32. THE FOUR COURTS AND SAINT SAVIOUR'S PRIORY

In about 1220 the Cistercians of Saint Mary's Abbey built a small church near the north end of the Old Bridge. They transferred it to the Dominicans,

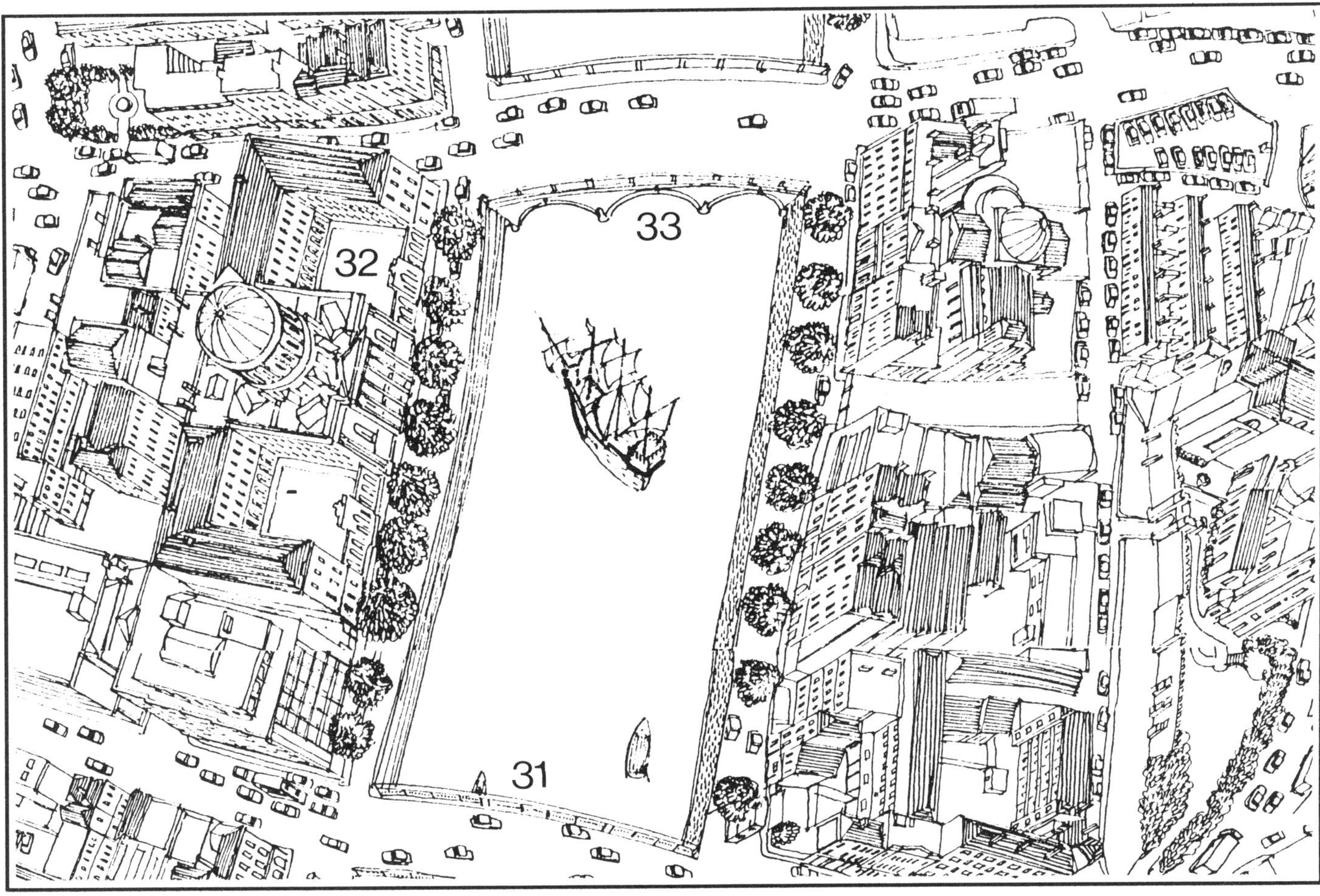

the order of Friars Preachers, in 1224, who built first a large church, and then a priory. This was probably in occupation by 1250, as in that year the city permitted the priory to have a 125mm diameter water main carried across the bridge, a stipulation being that, within the buildings, the diameter of each pipe should be reduced such "that its opening may be stopped by the insertion of a man's little finger." A fire that swept through Oxmantown in 1304 destroyed large parts of the buildings but these were quickly rebuilt. In 1317, Edward Bruce, who had been crowned King in Ireland at Dundalk the previous year, and Robert, his brother, King of the Scots, advanced on Dublin in an unsuccessful bid to take the city from the English. The citizens, led by their mayor Robert Nottingham, set about defending the city and, using the Church of Saint Saviour as a stone quarry, strengthened the river walls and blocked off the city gates. King Edward II later commended his people of Dublin for their loyalty, requiring at the same time that they rebuild the church. As he observed "although laws were squatted in warre yet nothwithstanding they ought to be revived in peace."

In 1539, in the time of Henry VIII, the priory was surrendered to the King. The church was once more demolished, this time with regal authority, and in about 1542 the remaining buildings were assigned to be the King's Inns, headquarters and lodgings for the legal profession. This occupancy continued within a steadily decaying fabric for nearly 250 years. In about 1775, by which time they had survived long enough to give their name to Inns Quay, the buildings were demolished to make room for the new Four Courts.

There had been a steady lobby for over a hundred years to take the courts out of the sundry cramped quarters they occupied inside the city walls. In 1683 a site was offered in Oxmantown, but a petition to the lord deputy was successful in blocking the move, the principal grounds being commercial: "if the courts be removed the heart of the cittie will be left destitute and many hundreds of families will be undone." In 1695 the courts were assembled under one roof, to be known later as the Old Four Courts, on a confined site tucked in between Christ Church and Skinners Row, in a building designed by William Robinson.

This was not a lasting solution and, in 1776, the Four Courts eventually crossed the river. In October that year the Earl of Harcourt, lord lieutenant, laid the first foundation stone for a vast new building, one of the largest the city had ever known, on the site of Saint Saviour's Priory. This ceremony inaugurated Thomas Cooley's work on the project. On the death of Cooley in 1784, James Gandon was engaged and the foundation stone for his work was laid in March 1786 by the Duke of Rutland, then lord lieutenant. The first court sittings in the Four Courts were in 1796. The buildings were completed in 1802, in the December of which year the Liffey floods that swept away the Ormonde Bridge inundated the main hall of the Courts, turning it, as John Carr wrote a few years later, into a Roman bath.

In June 1922, the Four Courts were bombarded with shells from across the river. The buildings were set on fire and extensively damaged. The reconstruction, which included the building of a new dome, was effected quickly, thus echoing the fourteenth century precedent, and was completed in 1931.

33. O'DONOVAN ROSSA BRIDGE

A person walking down Winetavern Street towards the Liffey two hundred years ago would have come upon the fronts of the houses in Pudding Row, a short street linking Merchants Quay and Wood Quay. These houses, some with yards or gardens, backed directly onto the river. Some fifty metres downstream, at the beginning of Wood Quay, was Ormonde Bridge.

In 1802 Ormonde Bridge fell down. Ten years later, in 1812, it was decided to build a replacement, not on the same site but opposite the end of Winetavern Street. In the process, part of Pudding Row was demolished and, by 1837, the whole of that street had been absorbed into a continuation of Wood Quay, with no houses on the bank of the river.

The precise site for the new bridge, which came to be called Richmond Bridge after the viceroy of the time, was a matter of controversy. A small, very influential group of citizens called for the bridge to be sited on the axis of the recently built Four Courts, to be approached by a splendid new avenue sweeping down to it on an embankment from High Street, crossing Cook Street with a bridge, and dividing Merchants Quay into two parts. The same group dismissed Winetavern Street as a modern artery because "the steepe at the west end of Christchurch is so great that no carriage can safely go up and down."

The planners prevailed and, in October 1812, George Knowles was awarded a contract to build the new bridge to a design prepared substantially by James Savage. In 1813, the Duchess of Richmond laid the foundation stone with a silver trowel costing £13/19s/11d presented to her to mark the occasion. The bridge was opened to traffic on Saint Patrick's Day in 1816.

It is recorded that, when the foundations were being excavated, the remains of two wooden boats, one containing a human skeleton, were found below the surface of the river bed.

The bridge has three stone arches and elaborate cast iron and stone balustraded parapets which continue along Inns Quay and across Father Mathew Bridge as an enrichment of the Four Courts' frontage. The six keystones in the arches of the bridge represent, facing downstream, Plenty, Anna Liffey, and In-

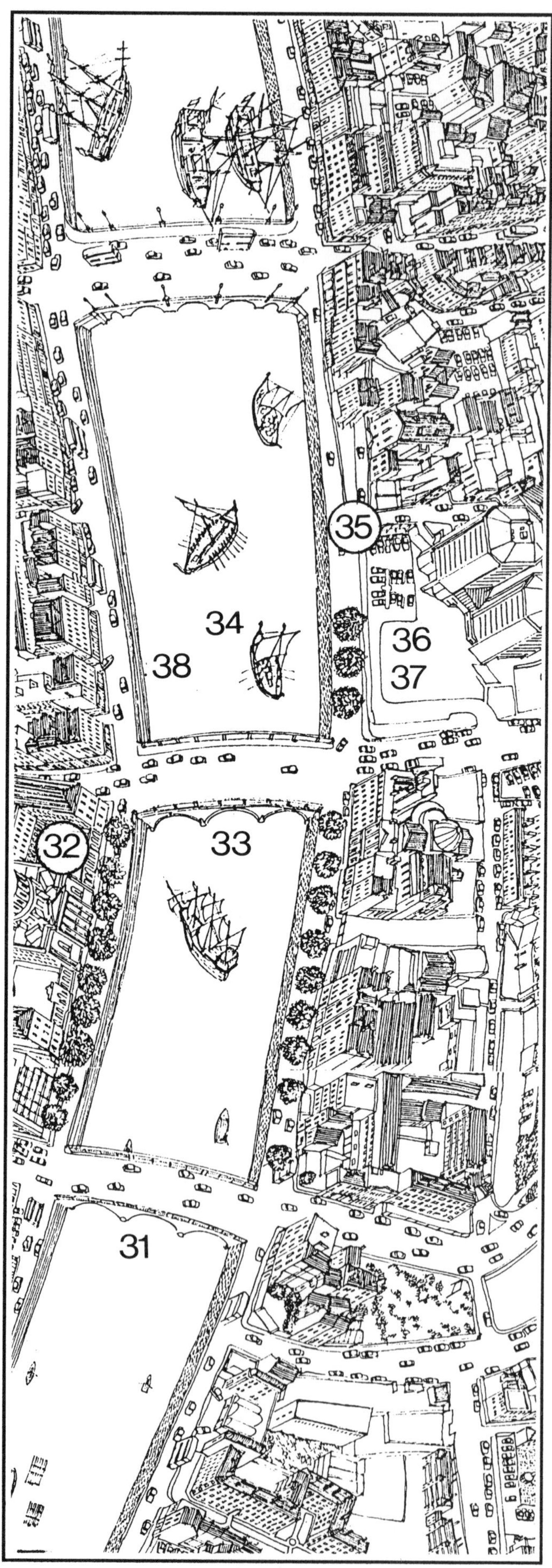

LOST BRIDGES

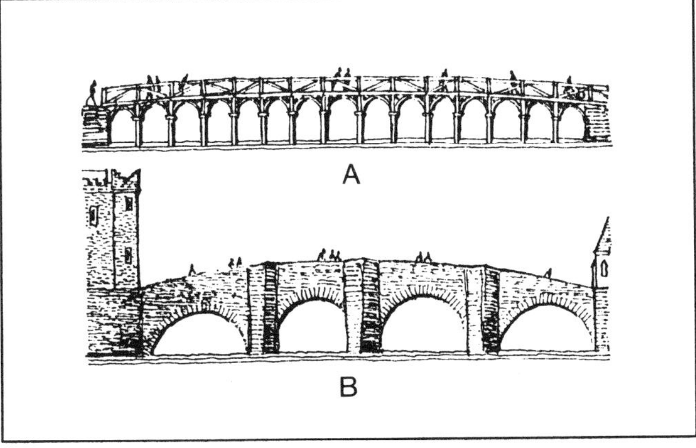

A: Typical early timber bridge
B: 'Old Bridge of Dublin' (1428-1816)

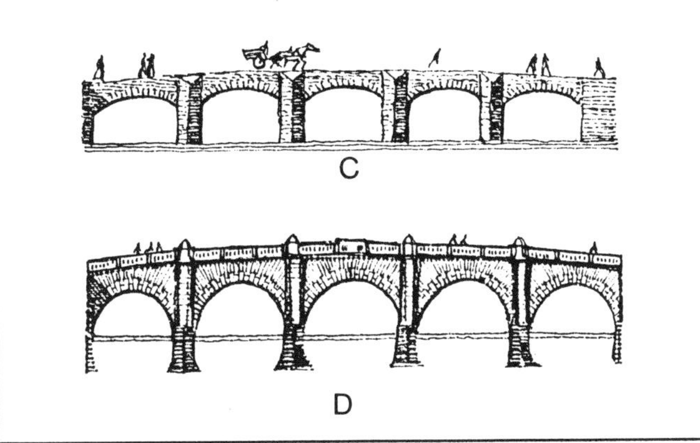

C: Ormonde Bridge (1684-1802)
D: Essex Bridge 1775, which replaced the bridge
built by Jervis in 1678.

dustry; facing upstream, Commerce, Hibernia, and Peace. They were carved by John Smyth, son of Edward Smyth, who had been the sculptor of the New Custom House river heads.

The name of the bridge was changed in 1922 to O'Donovan Rossa Bridge in commemoration of the Irish nationalist, Jeremiah O'Donovan Rossa (1831-1915).

34. ORMONDE BRIDGE

In 1682 Sir Humphrey Jervis built, at his own expense, a timber bridge across the Liffey at what was then the west end of Wood Quay, about fifty metres downstream of Winetavern Street. He was lord mayor of Dublin at the time and he named the bridge for the Duke of Ormonde, then in his second spell as lord lieutenant. After the completion of the bridge, an exercise in which railings had not apparently been thought necessary, the city required them to be provided, on both sides "to prevent people falling off the Bridge into the river." Despite this enhancement, the bridge, later stated to be of "injudicious construction", was condemned, and, in 1684, was demolished, to be replaced by a stone arched bridge of, it would appear, six spans. The new bridge may have had a lifting span. The circumstances are not clear.

An important commercial development of the time was the opening of public markets on the north bank of the river. One such was a hide market. It is recorded that this valuable, if nasally obtrusive, amenity could be accepted at the north end of the bridge, on Ormonde Quay "because the houses of most note where persons of quality do lodge" were at the quite distant east end of the quay. In 1756, following complaints about conditions on the Ormonde and Essex bridges, a man was appointed to keep them clean and free from beggars and fruit sellers. He was paid five shillings per week, out of which he was required to provide the necessary brooms and shovels at his own expense.

In 1752, Ormonde Bridge was in danger of collapse and in 1776 George Semple, engineer, architect, and builder, declared: "I do apprehend that within some very short time it must inevitably fall." This it did in a severe storm in December 1802. No new bridge was built on the site.

This crossing has sometimes been called Coal Quay Bridge.

35. TOWERS ON THE RIVER

In 1585, Sir John Perrott, lord deputy for Elizabeth I, ordered a survey to be made of the walls of the city. The walls were punctuated with towers or fortified houses, and six of these were on the riverside. These buildings formed part of the defences of the city, but were normally used as dwellings, stores, warehouses, prisons or meeting places, according to the need of the occupier at any time.

1. WILLIAM USHER'S HOUSE

This has been mentioned in the note on Usher's Island. The 1585 survey reported that here "the Liffie goethe hard by, and at every full sea, it floes up against the said wall [of Usher's house] being a spring tyde."

2. BRIDGE GATE OR OSTMANS GATE

This has been mentioned in the note on Father Mathew Bridge. The nine-metre high tower had two storeys, the upper being of timber. In plan it was 5.4 metres by 4.2 metres and its walls were 2.1 metres thick.

3. PRICKETT'S TOWER

First mentioned in the thirteenth century, this tower was located opposite Winetavern Street. When it first got its name, or what it was originally called, is not clear, but it was in Prickett's possession in 1585. It was a 10.2 metre high tower with a floor area of 9 metres by 7.2 metres, and it contained a timber loft and a turret.

4. FYAN'S CASTLE

First mentioned in the fourteenth century, this large building was located opposite Fishamble Street. It came into the possession of Richard Fyan in 1558, and in the middle of the seventeenth century came to be known as Proudfoot's Castle, at which time also it was used as a state prison. It was a 12.6 metre high four-storeyed structure, with a floor area of 11.4 metres by 6 metres, and 1.2 metre thick walls. It was probably demolished at the time that the quay, later to be known as Essex Quay, was opened, between 1680 and 1700.

5. FITZSYMON'S TOWER

Located about forty-five metres east of Fyan's Castle, this was a "small round tower without and square within." It was 6.6 metres high with walls about one metre thick, the floor area being 3.6 metres by 4.2 metres. It appears to have had two storeys, the upper being of timber. This tower became known as Case's Tower in the seventeenth century.

6. ISSOLDE'S TOWER

This fortified building was twelve metres high, round on the outside, and 5.4 metres square inside with two storeys and walls reaching a thickness of 2.7 metres. In 1558 it was let to the "master, wardens, and corporacion of the bakers." About fifty years later in 1604, this tower was leased to Jacob Newman for 119 years, and Speed, in his map of 1610, described it as Newman's Tower. It was located some forty metres from the south end of Essex (now Grattan) Bridge and it marked the eastern end of the early quays.

In 1577 Richard Stanihurst wrote of Issolde's Tower: "It took the name of 1a Beale Isoud, daughter of Anguish, King of Ireland. It seemeth to have been a castle of pleasure for the Kings to recreat themselves therein." Whilst this scarcely dates the first mention of the name, the tower in its prominent position overlooking the Poddle-Liffey confluence must have seemed of dateless antiquity. The demolition of the tower was sanctioned by the Council in 1681, but it would appear to have been identifiable, perhaps only by its stump, at the end of the eighteenth century.

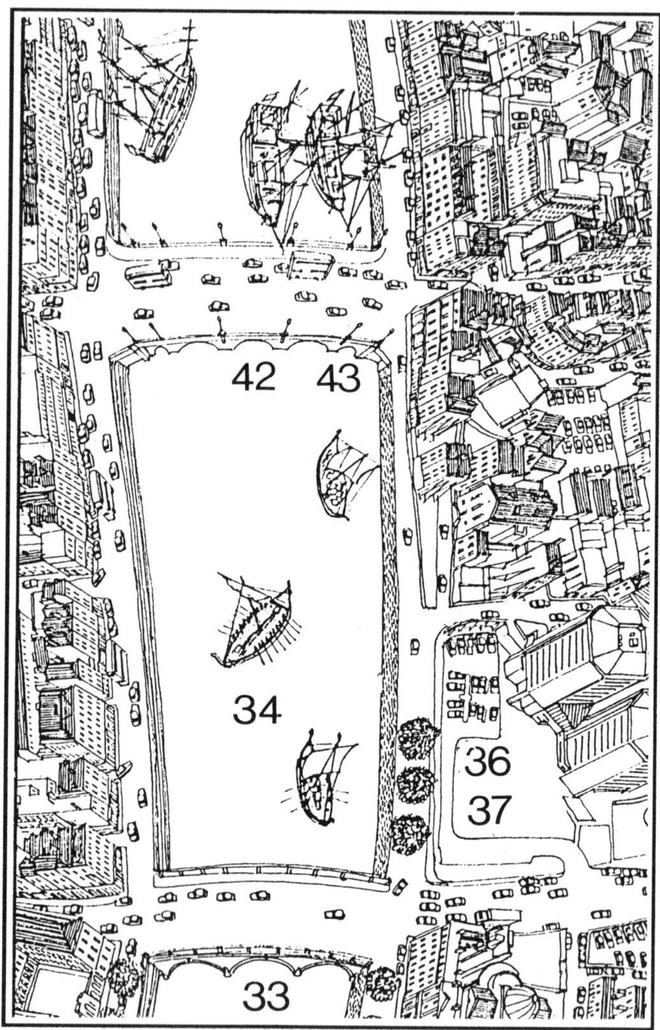

36. WOOD QUAY

The early town of Dublin was built largely on the ridge between the Poddle and the Liffey near Christchurch and down off the ridge to the river some fifteen metres below.

About fifty years after the Norsemen established their settlement, they built an earthen bank below the ridge to hold back the tide and make a place for loading and unloading their ships. This was the first Wood Quay, the oldest quay in Dublin. Later generations gradually increased the quay area by

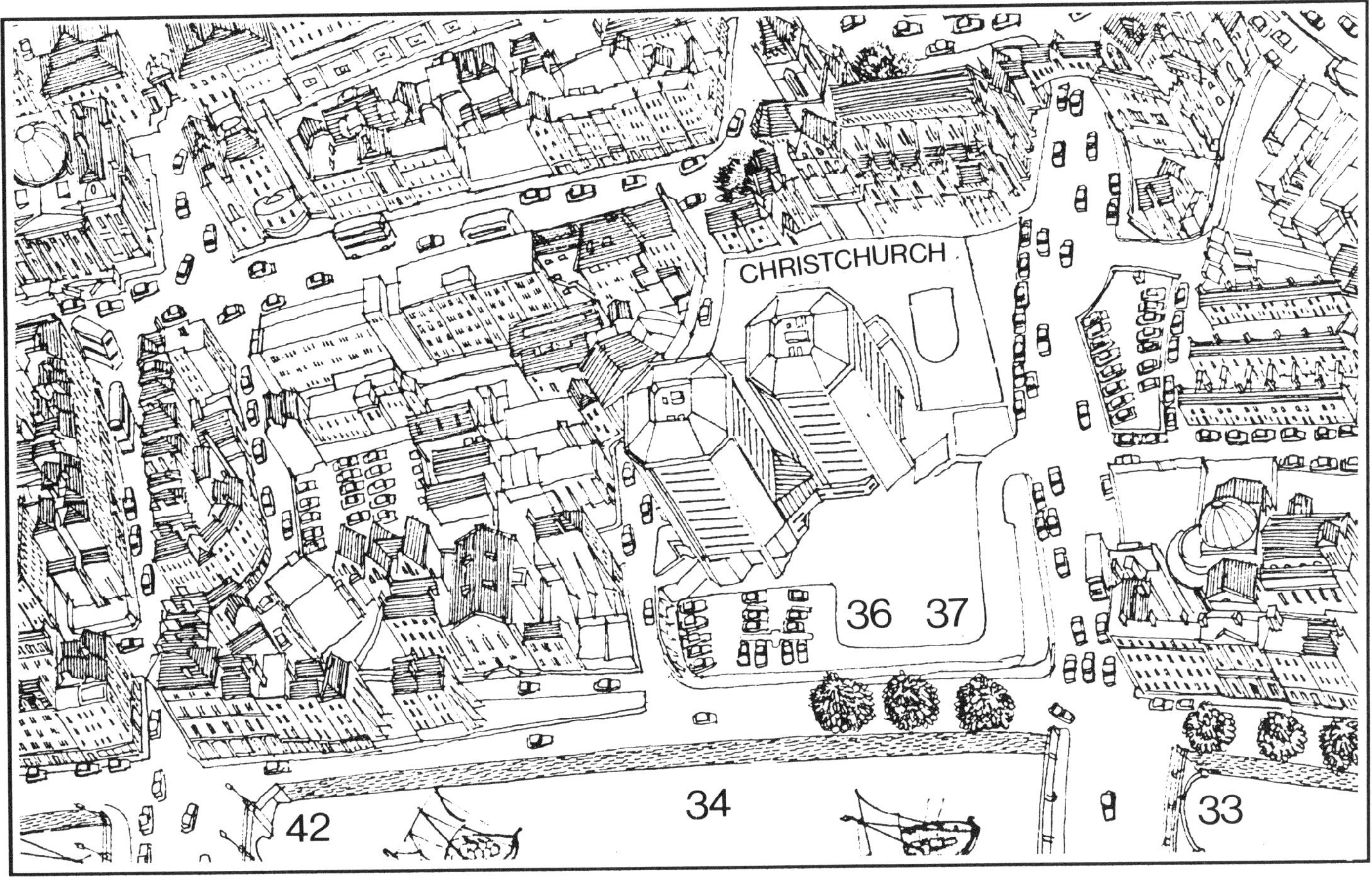

repeatedly building in front of the older work. The Anglo-Normans continued the process following their conquest of the city. By 1300, a stone wall had been built along what is today the land side of the Wood Quay thoroughfare. According as the area of dry land became larger, people moved into the parts behind the quay, building houses and workshops. Over the centuries the houses decayed and collapsed and others were built on top of them. Perseverance and skill have revealed a lot about how these many generations lived, and patience through yet another building life-cycle may bring further knowledge to some future generation.

Now, 700 years later, the river has been pushed back a little further, perhaps twenty metres, and the formation of Wood Quay is probably complete. The following notes on this quay during those seven hundred years relate primarily to a strip along the river probably about twice the length of the present Wood Quay.

In medieval times Wood Quay extended from Winetavern Street to Fishamble Street. Two major buildings — Prickett's Tower on the riverside and the Crane, a fourteenth-century forerunner to the Custom House, located in the corner formed by the quay and Winetavern Street — marked the upstream end of the quay. Fyan's, or Proudfoot's, Castle, known from about 1300, marked the downstream end. Later, it would be recorded that Wood Quay extended further downstream to Essex Bridge (until Essex

Quay, which had been formed between 1680 and 1700, was named as such after 1728); and during the eighteenth century and perhaps earlier, Pudding Row would block the quay between Ormonde Bridge and Winetavern Street. Fyan's Castle lay on what is today the land side of Essex Quay, a fact which enables one to visualise the position of the medieval quay. John Speed's map of 1610 shows the quay as described here, although one must wonder if the high unbroken wall shown by him is a correct representation.

During the seventeenth century, salients were gradually pushed out into the river beyond Speed's wall, at various points along the quay. In 1695 it was recorded that rubble from houses being demolished near New Gate was being used for the general widening of Wood Quay.

During that century, Wood Quay was a bustling place. The density of traffic using the adjacent Blind Quay to reach the river side contributed to the need for new access along Essex Quay. Edicts had to be issued prohibiting the use of the quay as a "warehouse" for heavy materials such as timber, planks, slates, millstones and paving stones. One part of the quay was the centre of the retail coal trade (hence the name Coal Quay sometimes used). In 1654 instructions were given for "timbringe the Wood Key as formerlie", which might suggest why the quay was so named. In 1642 the city found it necessary to order the replacement of "a jakes or common house of office beside

Fyan's castle"; and all this time a battle continued between the city fathers and people using the river as a rubbish dump. In 1578 owners of "oulde shippes and barkes which lieth at Wod Key" were warned "on their perill" to take them away. There could be as little as one metre of water at the quayside (presumably at high tide) and this was considerably influenced by random refuse disposal.

With the building of the first Essex Bridge (now Grattan Bridge) in 1678, and the removal of its lifting span in about 1684, access to Wood Quay for seagoing vessels ceased, and the quay became a wharf for the small lighters, barges, and gabbards that carried goods into the city from ships moored in the pools in the estuary. Wood Quay however continued as a waterside precinct, commercially busy and a popular place of residence. In 1726, it had for its security a watch-house manned by a constable and twelve men who, for the better execution of their duty, applied for and were given "a cage of wood" two-and-a-half metres square to be placed outside the watch-house to hold "idle strollers" securely "till they may be brought to justice in the morning."

Wood Quay remains to this day a place of civic significance. Rising over the area of the early banks and revêtments, tall twentieth-century offices, new quayside towers, have been built for the city administration.

37. GUNPOWDER EXPLOSION AT WOOD QUAY

In March 1597, a cargo of twenty-five tons of gunpowder was sent to Dublin. The vessel carrying this cargo anchored in one of the pools in the estuary and the powder, in firkins or casks, was brought upstream to the Crane in lighters. On 11 March the final delivery of seven tons was unloaded at Wood Quay in about 150 firkins for transport by road to Dublin Castle. Then, possibly because children playing with the firkins, or a horse with his shoe, struck a spark, the gunpowder exploded.

Reporting the incident to Sir Robert Cecil, Queen Elizabeth's secretary of state, Sir James Norris said (the text is given here with modern spelling): "Three of Sir George Bourchier's men that had the charge of it with the keeper of the Crane and all the labourers about it are perished; the ruin of the town is exceeding great, twenty houses by estimation, next adjoining, thrown to the ground, not any one house or church within the walls but in the tilings, small timbers and glass marvellously endamaged, and many in like sort in the suburbs. It is supposed that there are slain of all ages and sexes near two hundred; few English, nor any of account, but one of the Ratclyfes, master of a bark of Chester...Though the loss to her majesty be not great...yet is the mishap to be pitied and accounted a just plague of God for the sins of so

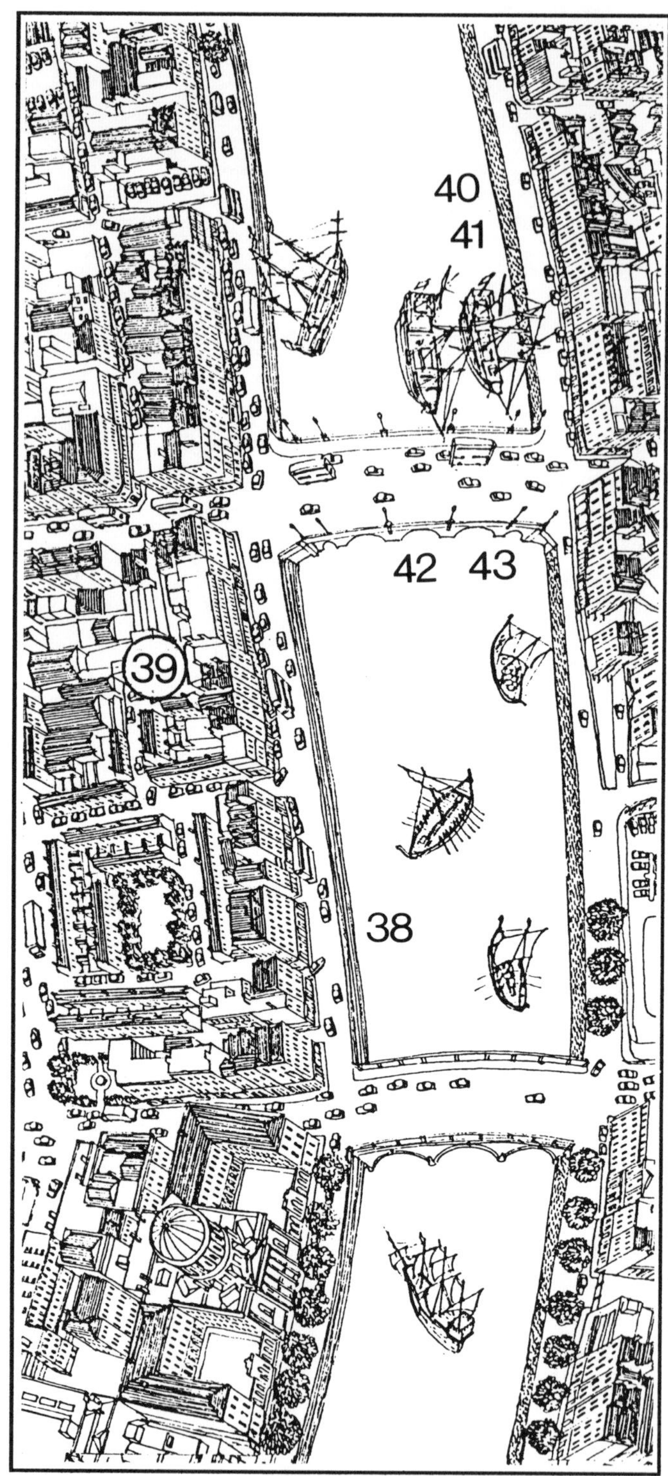

impious and ungrateful a people."

Later the Mayor recorded that "We the Mayor and Sherriffs of the city of Dublin, upon enquiry and examination, do find that there is of persons known, who fortuned to be in the last misfortune happened within the city of Dublin, lost to the number of six score, beside sundry headless bodies and heads without bodies that were found and not known."

38. THE BRADOGUE RIVER

The Bradogue was one of the three important tributaries of the medieval Liffey in Dublin. It lasted as a visible river just long enough to be shown by John Speed in his map of 1610 before gradually being built over. It appears on no later maps, although many stretches continued in the open air for 200 further years or more, and the first Ordnance Survey maps in 1838 plotted its course.

The Bradogue, also known as Bradock's Brook, rises near Fassaugh Road and Quarry Road in Cabra and flows south through Grangegorman, past the former Broadstone railway terminus, and along Halston Street, to discharge into the Liffey at Ormonde Quay. A branch probably flows east under North Brunswick Street, formerly called Channel Row.

The stretch of the north bank of the Liffey represented today by Upper Ormonde Quay was a tidal slob seamed with little creeks, rivulets and pools. At high tide it could occasionally have been inundated. One of the creeks, to the east, had much earlier been developed as a quay for Saint Mary's Abbey; and Speed shows that near the west end of the slob the Bradogue had its channel. At high tides, vessels could have sailed into creeks and channels to berth, and this, or the Abbey Quay, may account for the tradition that the Bradogue was at one time navigable.

As early as 1610, Pill Lane, the present Chancery Street and Mary's Abbey, was shown as linking this slob area to the Old Bridge, and it was probably there very much earlier as the way from Saint Mary's Abbey to the city. In 1629 a bridge called Bradocke Bridge carried the road to Finglas across the stream, and it is quite possible that this crossing, which was most likely at Constitution Hill, was also the site of the Bradogue stepping stones which are said to have given the Broadstone station its name.

39. SAINT MARY'S ABBEY

There are several variations of the name for this abbey, including Saint Mary of Ostmanby, and the House of the Blessed Virgin Mary near Dublin.

The Norse rulers of Dublin founded a Benedictine monastery on the north bank of the Liffey in 948. In 1139 it was transferred to the Cistercians. In the grants of land that followed the Norman conquest, Saint Mary's Abbey came into possession of most of the north-east of modern Dublin from their abbey in Oxmantown to the Tolka at Ballybough. In a most jealously guarded concession from the Crown, the abbey property was excluded from the city lands, and accounts tell of confrontations between the Mayor and the Abbot on the occasions of the riding of the city franchises.

There would seem to have been close association between the abbey, the Crown and the city governors.

In 1250 the abbey was active in a shipping trade with western Europe from its own quay, and enjoyed official support for this venture; throughout the ensuing centuries, the abbey apartments were used for meetings of the Council of State and to provide lodging for important visitors from England. It was at a meeting of the Council of State in the Chapter House of the abbey in 1534 that Silken Thomas Fitzgerald, the twenty-one-year-old son of the lord deputy, dramatically surrendered his sword of state to the Council, withdrew his allegiance to the Crown, and rose in rebellion against it.

In 1539 the abbey was surrendered into the hands of King Henry VIII. Four years later, in 1543, after 600 years as one of the most prestigious abbeys in Ireland, it was in use for stabling and as lodgings for the retinue of the Earl of Kildare.

Speed's map of 1610, drawn at a time when the buildings had apparently fallen into disuse, shows the polygonal enclosure of the abbey precinct, and suggests, through the small standing cross drawn near the northern entrance, the concept of medieval sanctuary that monasteries could offer to fugitives. During the seventeenth century the decay of the abbey buildings would continue, culminating in their use by Humphrey Jervis in 1678 as a quarry for stone for the building of the first Essex (now Grattan) Bridge.

Little remains of the abbey today except the handsome vaulted Chapter House in Meetinghouse Lane, and the medieval wooden statue of Our Lady of Dublin. Thrown out for burning in the sixteenth century, this statue was found again after many years and is now enshrined at the Carmelite church in Whitefriar Street.

A reconstruction drawing of St Mary's Abbey

40. THE RIVER PODDLE

The River Poddle, also known as the Sallagh, rises in Cookstown near Tallaght and flows into Dublin through Kimmage and Harold's Cross. From about 1250 the Poddle, augmented by water diverted from the Dodder, provided the water supply for the city. A natural course for the river in early times would have been from Harold's Cross by the west side of Clanbrassil Street to Saint Patrick's Cathedral and from there around the south and east of Dublin Castle and so into the Liffey. The needs of Saint Thomas's Abbey, however, and extensive use of the water for milling by the monks and others led to the diversion of the river and its subdivision into several streams.

The confluence of the Poddle and the Liffey was important in the earliest history of the city. The pool at the confluence was, possibly, the Black Pool or Dubh Linn that gave Dublin its name and there was always a harbour at this place. It was from here in 1534 that Archbishop Alen, fearing the anger of Silken Thomas Fitzgerald, took a boat for England, only to be cast ashore by storm at Clontarf and later captured in Artane by Fitzgerald's followers and "most inhumanely murdered."

Where it met the Liffey, the Poddle was in two branches, with a narrow island between them. Whether these were both natural is not clear. A water mill or mills, the King's Mill or Dames Mill, had been built east of the Castle as early as 1248, and the jumble of mill streams, dams, tail races, bridges and possibly some secure harbourage, suggests that one of the branches could have been made or at least developed by men. They could also have had the making of a waterfilled ditch outside the city walls in mind.

In 1606, Jacob Newman of Newman's Tower, whose name is stamped on the development of this area, purchased the slob land in the mouth of the Poddle. In 1610, John Speed shows it as a broad river mouth with the island between two streams. By 1621, this area had been reclaimed. In 1673, De Gomme's map shows the Liffey bank continuous, with only one branch of the Poddle entering it, roughly where it does today, opposite Swift's Row. The tidal flat east of the original confluence had become, as early as 1621, the site for a new quay, the Custom House Quay. By this time also a long stretch of the Poddle from near the north wall of the Castle towards the Liffey had gone underground, and the newly developed land north of Dame Street had become the location for a new Council Chamber and a depot for the Horse Guards. These were approached from Dame Street by, using their modern names, Crane Lane and Crampton Court, respectively. The Poddle flowed underground, as it still does, between these lanes.

The Dames Mills were described in 1694, three hundred years ago, as "now shutt up" but the area continued, at least into the nineteenth century, to be

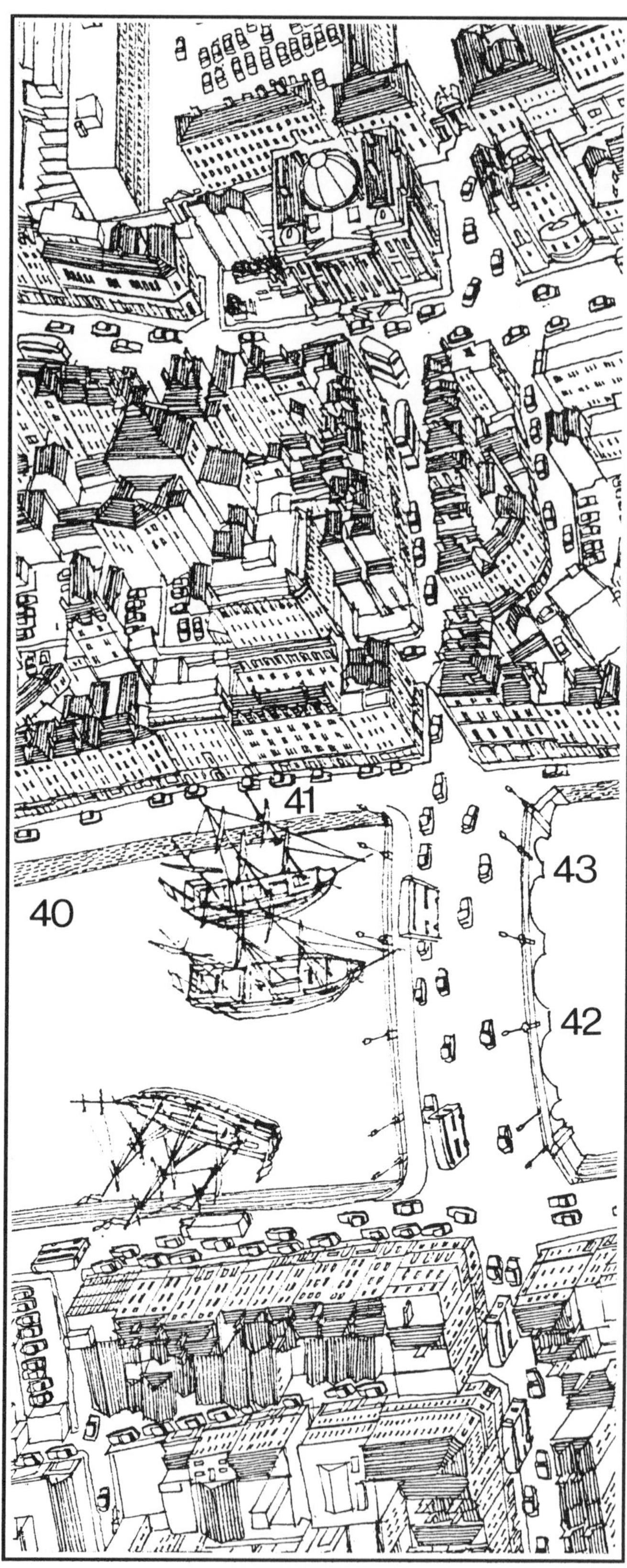

THE OLD CUSTOM HOUSE
Built in 1707 on the south bank, just
downstream of Grattan Bridge, to a
design by Thomas Burgh.

known by that name. The mouth of the Poddle went underground probably in 1707 with the building of the "Old Custom House". It did not, however, surrender its aura of mystery and ancient deeds. Some seventy years later, Sheriff Anthony King was knighted for capturing an escaping felon whom he chased through the Poddle tunnel; while in 1814 it is recorded that "a boy fell into the [Poddle] current from an arch which they were erecting over it in the Castle-yard. He was carried by the stream under Dame Street to the Liffey and was taken up just as he had emerged from the subterranean passage into the river."

41. THE OLD CUSTOM HOUSE

From early times, the import of merchandise into Dublin was controlled by the use of standard weights and measures held by "the Craner" at "the Crane". The principal crane in those days was at Wood Quay. In 1621, in the reign of James I, the official place of entry for merchandise was moved to a new Custom House Quay, just downstream of the present Grattan Bridge, and customs facilities were established there. De Gomme's map of 1673 shows this quay. The merchants, however, were not satisfied with the accommodation provided for them either in 1621 or later, after the Restoration.

In 1707 a new custom house, now known as the Old Custom House, was built on the Custom House Quay. A four-storeyed building, sixty metres long, was designed by Thomas Burgh to form the south side of the quay, and Tudor shows this in his drawing of 1753. The quay was now approached by steps from Essex Bridge and by a secured gateway from Essex Street.

It must already have been clear however, that the Port of Dublin could not be maintained so far upstream in a narrow tidal river. The crowding of ships in the channel in a block four ships long by eight ships wide was intolerable, although not without humour to the onlooker. Access to one ship was by way of another, and the master of the "Nelly" of Bordeaux was reported as having pumped wine out of the hold of his ship which he had never put into it!

As the century wore on, agitation for a new port downstream and a new custom house grew. Although there was predictably strong opposition to the move, expressed with lampoons and pamphlets rather than the knives and cudgels of Bloody Bridge a hundred years earlier, the decision to move the port east of the city was taken. In 1791 the Old Custom House, which had begun to show its age structurally some twenty years before, was closed. It was used briefly as a military post in 1798 and for some years later. The building was demolished during the nineteenth century and replaced by Dollard's printing house and the Clarence Hotel.

42. GRATTAN BRIDGE

Also known as Essex Bridge and Capel Street Bridge, this is the third oldest bridge site on the Liffey in Dublin. In 1676 Humphrey Jervis, using stone quarried from the ruins of Saint Mary's Abbey, began to build the first Essex Bridge and it was opened to traffic in 1678. Named for the viceroy, Arthur Capel, Earl of Essex, the main purpose of the bridge was to open a new route to the north bank of the river where Jervis owned land, in and around the present Capel Street. The bridge had seven spans, six of them stone arches and the seventh a timber lifting span. In December 1687 during a great flood on the river, one pier of the bridge collapsed. "At this time," it was reported, "there happened to be a Hackney-coach driving over the Bridge, but providentially there was no Body in the Coach and as they were just on the Crown of the Arch, the Bed of the River under that pier being carried away by the Floods, the Pier fell down and so down came the Arch, Coach, Coach-man and two Horses, and all together were swept down to the Watering-slip. The Man clung fast to the Coach-box, sometimes under and sometimes above Water, till they came to the Slip, where one of the Horses broke his Traces and swam out, but the Man and the other Horse were drowned."

The bridge was soon repaired but somewhat crudely, and at about this time the lifting span was replaced by a seventh stone arch. Boatmen who wished to sail upstream to Wood Quay or Merchants Quay were forced to "make their masts to strike." In 1722 a statue of King George I was erected on a pedestal upstream of the bridge, and this statue features as a vignette on Charles Brooking's map of 1728.

Less than thirty years later, in 1751, possibly due in part to the deflexion of flood water by the pedestal, the bridge was again "in a decaying and ruinous condition," and had to be closed to the public. It was demolished in 1753 and a new bridge, the second Essex Bridge, was completed in 1755, to a design by George Semple, who would later describe his work in his *Treatise on Building in Water* published in 1776. This was a handsome five-span stone arch bridge with a quite pronounced rise at the centre. Semple, knowing the menace of Liffey floods for bridge foundations, declared at the outset that his bridge would "last as long as the little adjacent mountain called Sugar-loaf Hill", a claim which holds true to date.

Essex Bridge, in the centre of city activity, became a profitable stand for stall-holders by day and a place for mayhem by night; it was reported to the Dublin Assembly in 1763 that "Essex Bridge is subject to many mischiefs at night." Attempts to banish the stall-holders, which were made from time to time, would appear to have been unsuccessful, if we are to listen to Zozimus who, during the 1830s, frequently stood on the bridge to declaim, amongst other topics, about the wife of Dicky the Yeoman,

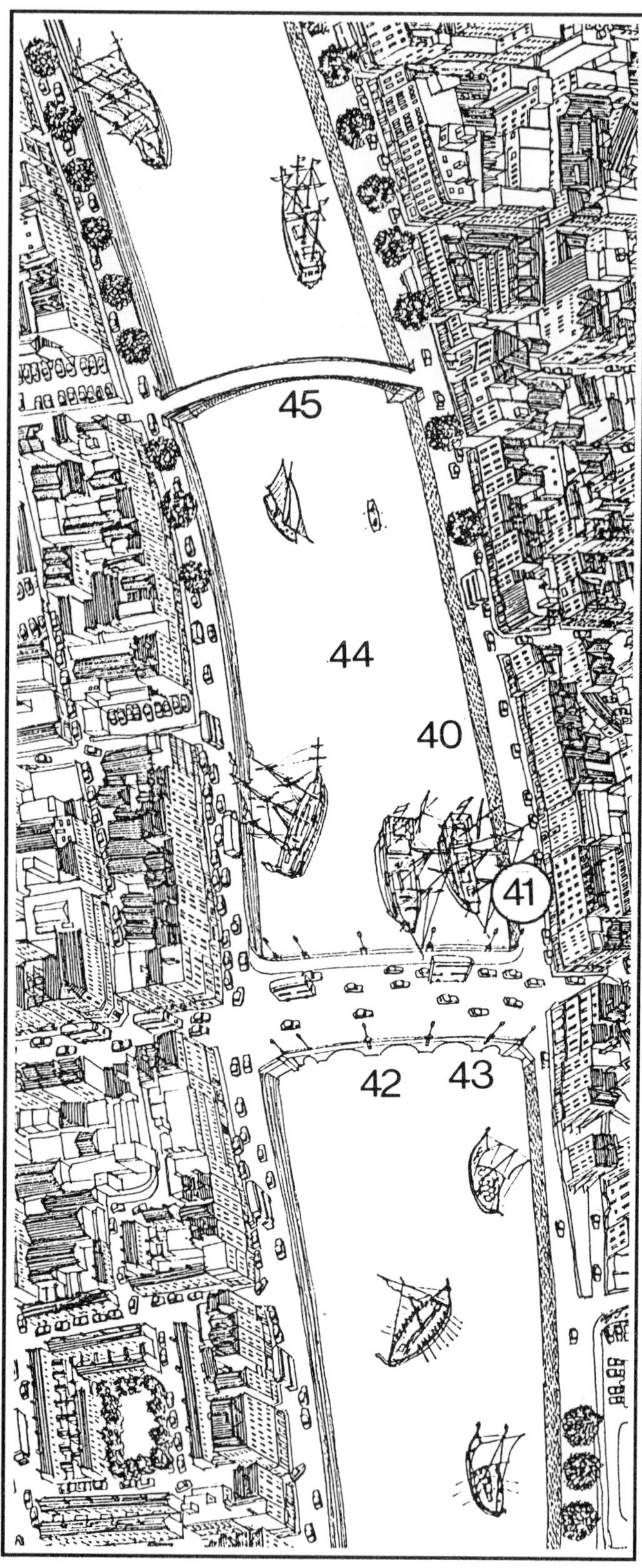

GEORGE I AND ESSEX BRIDGE

On Essex Bridge she strained her throat
And six-a-penny was her note.

In 1872 it was decided to widen the bridge and remove the hump, to have it run at a uniform slope from one quay to the other. Bindon Stoney designed the reconstruction using Semple's foundations (and so underwrote Semple's claim) and built a new bridge with flatter arches and some changes at the ends to accommodate new uses for the quays.

The new bridge, now re-named Grattan Bridge, is admired more for its efficiency than for its elegance, and the fact that the south end is nearly a metre higher than the north to suit the quay levels does not help.

An inscription on a plaque on the bridge reads:

Essex Bridge
Erected 1755
Rebuilt by the Dublin Port and Docks Board 1875
Renamed
Grattan Bridge
Right Honble. Peter Paul McSwiney, J.P. Lord
Mayor
Robert Warren, D.L. , J.P. High Sheriff
Bindon B. Stoney , Engineer
W.J. Doherty, Contractor.

43. EQUESTRIAN STATUE OF KING GEORGE I AT ESSEX BRIDGE

On 1 August, 1722 the City Council unveiled an equestrian statue, slightly larger than life-size, of King George I on a stone pedestal upstream of Essex Bridge. The statue was sculptured by John van Nost the Elder, and is shown as a vignette on Charles Brooking's map of 1728. The unveiling ceremony was elaborate, with a company of grenadiers being in attendance "from seven o'clock in the morning till the corporations marched over the bridge."

In 1753 George Semple decided that the position and shape of the pedestal were a danger to the stability of the bridge, and, in his reconstruction, had the statue and pedestal removed.

The statue next appeared in the front garden of the Mansion House with an inscription that read: "Be it remembered that at the time when rebellion and disloyalty were the characteristics of the day, the loyal Corporation of the city of Dublin re-elevated this statue of the first monarch of the illustrious House of Hanover, Jonas Paisley and William Henry Archer, Sheriffs, Anno Domini 1798."

Despite a request to make the statue a central feature in Fitzwilliam Square in 1815, it remained in Dawson Street where it was seen by William Thackeray during his visit to Dublin in 1842. He would later write, somewhat sourly, that he had seen "close at hand and peering over a paling, a statue of our blessed sovereign George II" (*sic*), adding "how absurd these pompous images look, of defunct majesties, for whom no breathing soul cares a halfpenny."

Again the statue disappeared from public view, and was not to re-appear in Ireland. In 1937 it was bought for the Barber Institute of Fine Arts at the University of Birmingham, in front of which it now stands on a three-metre high pedestal. An inscription on the pedestal reads: "This statue of George I by John van Nost the Elder was erected in Dublin in 1722 and bought for the Barber Institute in 1937."

44. STEADFAST DICK

A reef of rock known as Steadfast Dick, or Standfast Dick, which projected through the bed of the Liffey near Swift's Row, was for many centuries a hazard to shipping sailing upriver to the quays in the city. In evidence given to an Enquiry examining a proposal to build a new custom house and to move the centre of shipping activity downstream to below a proposed new crossing (Carlisle, later O'Connell Bridge), it was reported that "in 1770 a ship richly laden struck on Steadfast Dick in going up to the Custom House and both ship and cargo were very much damaged." In 1773 another vessel, the *Dolly*, was wrecked on the reef.

In 1776 the City Council was vigorously engaged, through its Ballast Office committee, in the removal of Steadfast Dick. It may be supposed that part of the reason for the exercise lay in the fact that it was possible to use the quarried stone, always a costly material, in works at the Great South Wall. It would surely have become apparent by then that a new bridge was almost certain to be built downstream, and that the use of the Old Custom House Quay by sea-going vessels would then end.

It has been suggested that there was a ford across the Liffey downstream of the Ath Cliath. If so, it may have made use of the Steadfast Dick reef.

45. THE HA'PENNY BRIDGE

The official name for this crossing is the Liffey Bridge; to the people of Dublin it is the Ha'penny Bridge.

It was built as a toll bridge, probably to replace the Bagnio Ferry, and was opened on 19 May 1816. It was paid for by William Walsh, lessee of the ferries, with the support of John Claudius Beresford. Permission had been given to build on the condition that the toll for crossing the bridge would not exceed one halfpenny, which was then the ferry toll; this toll was collected on the bridge until 1916.

The bridge is a single cast iron span with three arched ribs. Each rib was cast in six segments in Shropshire, and the eighteen segments with all the

necessary extra bracing pieces were then floated down the Severn and shipped from Bristol to Dublin for assembly. It is a handsome bridge of more than usual interest, and is one of the significant heritage items in the built environment of Ireland.

For a short time, admirers of the Duke of Wellington, victor at Waterloo in 1815, called the bridge the Wellington Bridge. There is little evidence that he was particularly interested and quite soon the name was dropped. There were others who believed the name of the bridge should be associated with Beresford, whom they did not admire. Their opinion was that the shape of the bracing lamp-holder at the crown of the bridge would make appropriate the name "Triangle Bridge", as a compliment "to its founder for his exploits in 1798 upon a certain machine called the Triangle."

In 1912 the bridge became a focus for discussion when Hugh Lane proposed that it be removed and a picture gallery built in two pavilions on a new stone arched bridge on the same site. He had support from Lady Gregory and William Butler Yeats; and he enjoyed the advice of the noted English architect, Sir Edwin Lutyens, who prepared sketches and would have been happy to design the new bridge and gallery "in exchange for an Old Master" by way of fee. The project lapsed with Lane's death on the Lusitania in 1915. He and his supporters had been vociferous in denouncing the ugliness of the metal bridge. They may, however, have based their dislike not on the proportions of the structure but rather on the use of its railings and toll houses as supports for unsubtle advertisements for pills and ointments, chicken meal and dog cakes. Advertisements of this kind can spoil even the most elegant of bridges.

46. HOGGEN GREEN

Hoggen Green was a large unfenced area of pasture bounded roughly by the Poddle, the Liffey, the Stein, and the present line of Dame Lane or Exchequer Street and Suffolk Street. The Poddle is taken here as representing the eastern boundary of the pre-Norman town. The Liffey was tidal, so the north side of the Green was, at high tide, possibly no more than a low grassy verge and, at low tide, a mud or shingle bank sloping down to the channel of the river. At high tide, the Liffey tideway lapped "the old Shore" at the Bank of Ireland in College Green. Much of the area we know today as Westmoreland Street and D'Olier Street was then almost certainly regularly inundated. The Stein boundary, beginning near the junction of Suffolk Street and Grafton Street, passed down by the west elevation of Trinity College and joined the Liffey near the Long Stone. Much of this east boundary was a waterlogged area, known as the "bogge" or the "ditches". The south boundary was indefinite. The Thingmount or Thingmote, so named by

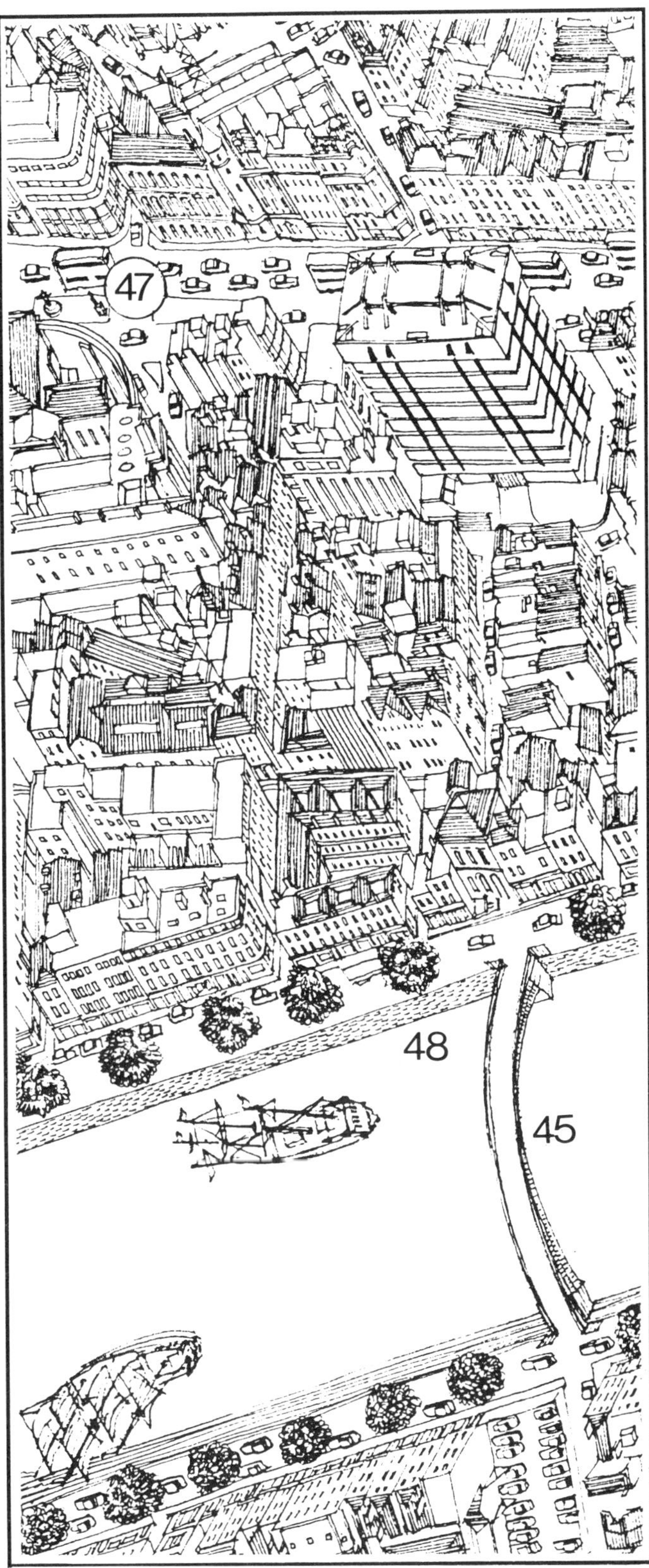

the Norsemen, was raised just across Suffolk Street from Saint Andrew's Church on the first slope rising from the river plain, and this is generally taken as having been on Hoggen Green.

The Green was certainly in use during the Norse period in Dublin. There is evidence of its having been a burial ground for some hundreds of years; and in 1146, shortly before the Anglo-Norman conquest, the convent of Saint Mary de Hogges was founded there "in a village called Hogges". The origin of this name is the word "hogge" which relates to sepulchral mounds, which did exist on the Green. In due course up to the seventeenth century, the area would be variously called Hoggin, Hoggen Butts, Hog's Green, Hogging Greene, Hogan's Green, Hog and Butts and the Howe.

In late medieval times, Hoggen Green was an open common, controlled by the city and its overlords, to be disposed of, as time went on, to developers. These would include for instance the builders of the thirteenth-century Monastery of the Holy Trinity (Saint Augustine's), and of Carey's Hospital, later to develop into the Bank of Ireland.

Access to Hoggen Green from the city was through the Dames Gate and the Blind Gate. There were two exits to the east. One followed the high-water shore, hugging the north side of All Hallows Priory and passing into the district of Lazers Hill. The other followed what may have been the prehistoric shore line around the Provost's House in Trinity College by the south, past Saint Patrick's Well and so by Lincoln Place and Denzille Lane towards the delta of the Dodder.

In considering the uses to which Hoggen Green was put, one might begin by recalling how long it survived as a communal entity, probably nine hundred years from 1700 back to 800, or even further. At the beginning it was a haunt for rabbits and seagulls, used as pasturage and to some extent as a place of burial. In the twelfth century with the foundation of Saint Mary's and All Hallows, its use as a cemetery may well have ceased. While the battle of Hoggen Green could have been fought amongst burial mounds, it is unlikely that the overlord, Henry II, would have chosen to spend the winter of 1171-72 in a temporary palace built on the site of a working graveyard.

From 1170 onwards, the Green was being used as a pasture, as a place of recreation for the citizens, and as a dumping ground for refuse. Archery was practised, hence the name Hoggen Butts. Skittles and bowling were other pastimes; and indeed it was to be complained in 1621 that strangers rather than Dubliners were making the profit from "the inrayled bowling place in the Hoggen Greene."

Indiscriminate grazing was frowned on. "Forasmoche" an order of 1585 stated "as swyne unringed uppon Hoggen Grene are noysome and hurtful to the same ... and also that the swyne coming on the strond hyndreth greatly thincrease of the fyshe", it was agreed that one Edward Peppard should "pond [impound] any such swyne coming on the strond." A par-allel injunction forbade the retting of flax. The disposal of night soil and animal manure was care-fully controlled. An edict of 1571 issued the civic instruction that "all dounge that shalbe caryed to the saide greane [shall be placed] in the greate holl by All Hallowes." At the time, All Hallows priory was a dere-lict site owned by the city and not yet donated for a university.

John Speed shows that, in 1610, the north side of today's Dame Street had been built on from the city walls near the Olympia Theatre about as far as the Central Bank, that there had been some building in Exchequer Street, and that there were about half-a-dozen isolated buildings dotted around the area. The development of Hoggen Green was to proceed very quickly during the seventeenth and early eighteenth centuries. So fast was the process that Brooking on his map of 1728 could show the whole area largely built up, with the street pattern very much as we know it today, except along the bank of the Liffey and on the major approaches to the river where the street system we now have was then still in the future.

The name Hoggen Green was also falling into disuse at this time. In 1700, a lease was granted by the city for a part of "Hoggen Greene, alias Colledge Greene", whereas in 1728 Brooking names the east-ern end of Dame Street simply as Colledge Greene. In 1737 a reference in a roll of city rents to both Hoggen Green and College Green is the last use of the name in Gilbert's *Calendar of the Ancient Records of Dublin*. It is likely that by 1800, close on a thousand years after its first use, the name of Hoggen Green had lost currency.

47. THE BATTLE OF HOGGEN GREEN

About the feast of Pentecost in 1171, Askulv the Norseman, former governor of Dublin, with "his mind inflamed by a desire for vengeance" because of his de-feat and ignominious flight from the city the previous year, sailed up the Liffey with a great fleet, to recap-ture Dublin from the Normans. Landing probably along Lazers Hill, he had with him Norse allies from Scandinavia, the Orkney Islands and the Isle of Man.

When Askulv's army sallied forth from their ships led by one John the Wode, "they were warlike figures clad in mail in every part of their body after the Dan-ish manner. Some wore long coats of mail, others iron plates skilfully knitted together, and they had round red shields protected by iron round the edge."

Crossing the Stein bog, they advanced across Hoggen Green and attacked the city "against the east-ern gate, towards Saint Mary's gate." Miles Cogan, the city governor, made a sortie to meet them poss-ibly near the present statue of Thomas Davis, but was forced to retreat again into the city. At this juncture, Richard Cogan, his brother, who had left the city by

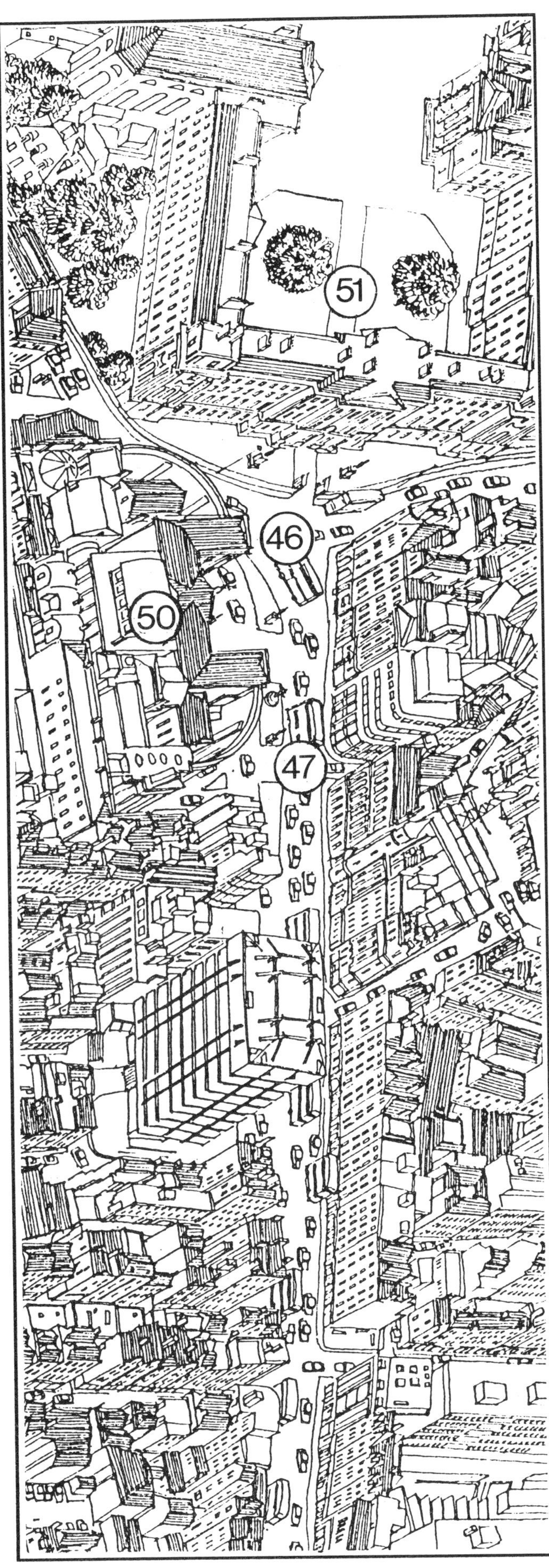

a southern gate came down, perhaps by South William Street:

"Richard came
Before that they were perceived
Upon the guard that was behind;
Loudly he shouted
Richard thereupon shouts
'Strike, valiant knights'
And the barons with great force
Threw themselves into the throng."

The battle was furious and ended with the rout of the Norsemen, both on the Hoggen Green, and in their boats as they tried to escape. John the Wode slew nine or ten of the enemy that day, hacking off the leg of one at the thigh with a single stroke of his axe, before himself falling to the sword of, probably, Walter de Ridelisford. Askulv was captured and beheaded.

During the whole of the day-long battle, Gillamocholmog, ruler of the "lands about the Dodder", son-in-law of Dermot Mac Murrough, brother-in-law of Strongbow, and in thrall to Cogan, watched impassively from a vantage point near the Thingmount. He had been ordered by Cogan to stay out of the battle until needed. He and his followers were eventually called in only to augment the rout, and join in the pursuit to the ships at the end of the day.

48. THE BAGNIO SLIP

Fownes Street, Upper and Lower, today runs from Dame Street to Wellington Quay. It will be noticed that the downhill slope of the street ends where it crosses Temple Bar and that one must walk slightly uphill along Fownes Street Lower to reach Wellington Quay. This rise is man-made and relatively new, dating from the making of the quay early in the nineteenth century. Before then the street continued downhill to end in the tideway of the Liffey, a little distance upstream of the Ha'penny Bridge and Fownes Street Lower. This was the Bagnio Slip. The name dates at least from the sixteenth century and may have been associated with a public bath house in the vicinity.

One of the river ferries crossed from steps at the Bagnio Slip, and the slip itself was a busy street. William Coats, a warden of the Holy Trinity Guild of merchants lived there in 1767. John Rocque the cartographer, who hints at the activity in this area in his map of 1756, would have been well placed to observe it, as he lodged almost directly across the river on Bachelors Walk during his stay in Dublin.

49. O'CONNELL BRIDGE

Even before the rebuilding of Essex (now Grattan) Bridge in 1755, agitation to move the port of Dublin downstream and to build a new custom house had begun. It was planned, partly as a corollary, to make a new bridge east of Essex Bridge. There was strong resistance. In 1750, for instance, a public notice appeared:

"Advertisment — The Freeholders, Merchants, and Traders of this City, who are willing to joyn in Application to Parliament against the intended Bridge over the Liffy are desired to meet at the Guild Hall in the Tholsel on Tuesday the 3rd of this Instant April 1750 at Ten o'clock in the Morning.

Printed by James Carson, at the Bagnio Slip on Temple Bar."

The years that followed saw the issue of many outspoken pamphlets addressed to an individual, or individuals, who might hope to profit from the new bridge at the expense of the city. Perhaps this resistance delayed the project but in 1786 work began on a new bridge on the axis of Gardiner's Mall (now Upper O'Connell Street), to a design by James Gandon. The foundation stone was laid by John Beresford in 1791 and the bridge was completed in 1794, and named for the lord lieutenant, the Earl of Carlisle. It was a simple three-spanned masonry structure with a slight rise, with the keystones in the arches sculptured by Edward Smyth.

Quite soon it would be used as a site for a gallows in the rising of 1798, Doctor John Esmonde being particularly remembered as one of those hanged there. At the same time Westmoreland Street and D'Olier Street were being opened to the south, and Drogheda Street would soon be widened to extend the spacious width of Gardiner's Mall down to the riverside from the north.

By about 1850 it was recognised that Carlisle Bridge was too narrow. In 1880 it was rebuilt, without a rise and about three times as wide as before. At this time the name of the bridge was changed to commemorate Daniel O'Connell (1775-1847), the Liberator, who continues impassively to observe his bridge from the great statue at its north end. A bronze plaque on the bridge carries the inscription

CARLISLE BRIDGE

BUILT 1794

REBUILT BY THE DUBLIN PORT AND DOCKS

BOARD 1880

RENAMED

O'CONNELL BRIDGE

BY THE MUNICIPAL COUNCIL 1880

RIGHT HONBLE EDMUND DWYER GRAY

M.P.LORD MAYOR

JAMES W. MACKEY. KNT D.L. HIGH SHERIFF

BINDON B.STONEY . ENGINEER

W.J.DOHERTY. CONTRACTOR

The choice of the new name was not without controversy, and it has been suggested that behind the bronze plaque there will be found the name Carlisle Bridge incised in the stone of the balustrade.

On the occasion of the thirty-first International Eucharistic Congress held in Dublin in 1932, the solemn benediction that concluded the ceremonies of the Congress was given from an altar erected on O'Connell Bridge.

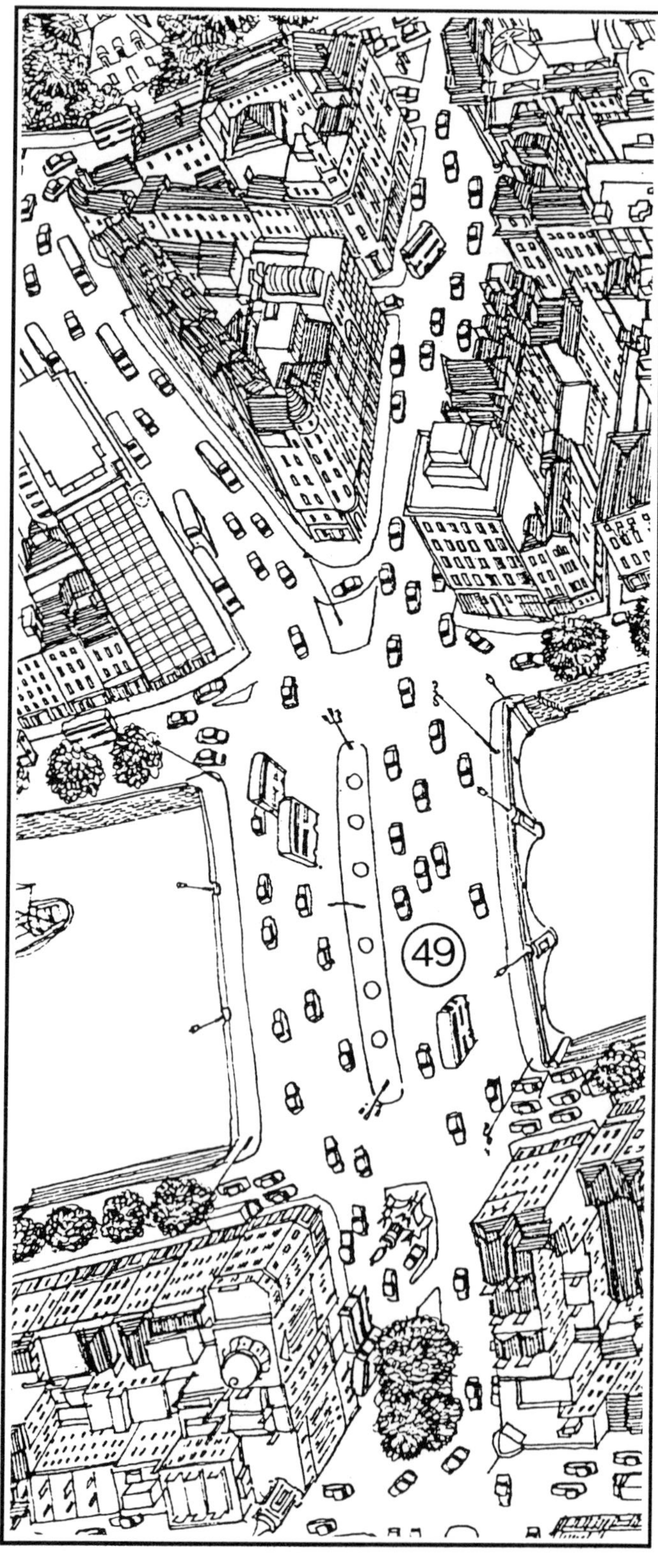

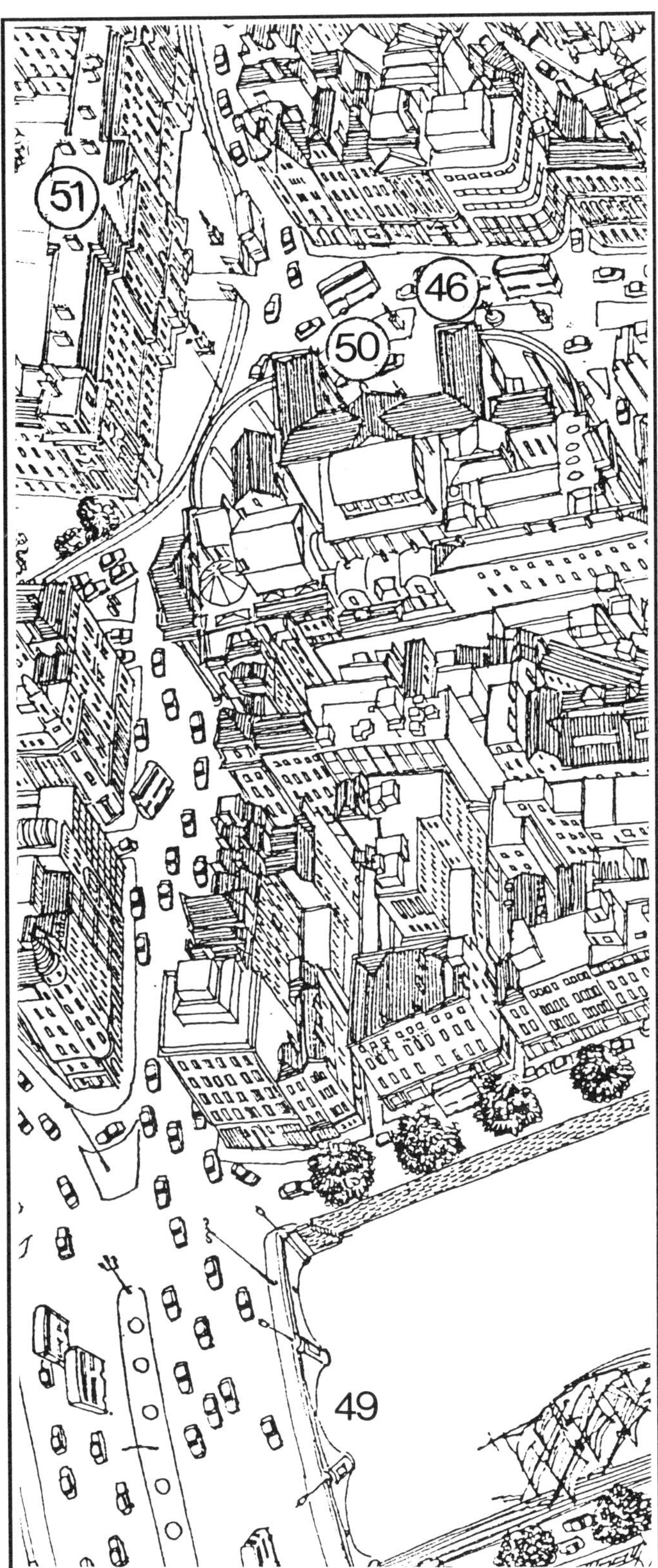

50. THE BANK OF IRELAND ON COLLEGE GREEN

One might wonder why the Bank of Ireland on College Green should be included in a set of notes on the River Liffey. It is now 200 metres or more from the nearest point of the river and to a passer-by would seem completely removed from it. If, however, one looks at John Speed's map and recalls the tide rising in the little river Stein adjacent, the position of Carey's Hospital, which is on roughly the same site as the bank, is seen to be more vulnerable. Indeed, storm-driven high tides would probably have lapped around it.

The sequence of building at this place, which here is taken generally from Gilbert's *Parliament House, Dublin* has been as follows:

At the end of the sixteenth century, Sir George Carey was given land on Hoggen Green to build a hospital for the relief of poor, sick and maimed soldiers. In 1603 Carey became lord deputy and offered to sell to the government the building and lands, which in 1606 were described as "a large mansion with a gatehouse, a garden, and plantations" which extended to the river bank. On their declining to purchase, the property passed through various hands to Sir Arthur Chichester, also a lord deputy, and agent for the crown in the Plantation of Ulster. He gave it the name of Chichester House and lived there until 1615. On his death in 1624, the house passed through some vicissitudes and several tenants to emerge again as the location for the first meeting of parliament in 1661, after the Restoration.

In 1728, having been used as a parliament house and being in a ruinous condition, it was demolished, and in 1729 the foundation stone for a new parliament house was laid by Hugh Boulter, Archbishop of Armagh. The new building, on generally the same site, was to the design of Captain Edward Lovett Pearce (1699-1733), a member of the Irish parliament. This parliament house, completed in 1731, was the scene of the debates on the proposed union of Ireland and Great Britain in 1799-1800, after which it ceased to be a parliament house. In 1803, however, it was still in the service of government as a military post during the rising of Robert Emmet. In 1802, it had been sold to the Bank of Ireland, which in 1804 began its adaptation for its present use, under the direction of Francis Johnston.

During this 200-year period, the Liffey tide was pushed back from Hoggen Green, or College Green as it was now being called. In 1673 Bernard de Gomme shows in his map that "the ground taken in from the sea" by Willliam Hawkins and Henry Aston, two of the earliest of the city developers, had established roughly the present high-tide line on the south bank of the river from Temple Lane to Hawkins Street, and it was now possible to describe only the west side of the parliament house as the "Old Shore", as a lease map of 1734 showed.

In 1783, the Irish House of Lords decided on the development of new apartments in the parliament house, to be approached by an entrance facing east. James Gandon prepared the design. It is of interest to see today that the steps he required to lead to this eastern entrance door, and the pedestals for the columns in the east portico, have been partially buried by the raising of the adjacent streets and footpaths.

51. TRINITY COLLEGE AND ALL HALLOWS PRIORY

One of the earliest drawings that shows a building in Dublin in its relation to the River Liffey is the Hatfield Plan made probably in 1592, eighteen years before Speed's map.

In 1166 the Priory of All Hallows or All Saints was founded by Dermot MacMurrough for the canons of the order of Arrouaise. It was on the east edge of Hoggen Green, between the Green and Lazers Hill. Its north wall, and possibly the main gate, faced the Liffey, and storm-driven tides would flood the shore road that passed along that north wall on its way to Lazers Hill. The priory had its own mill, driven either by tidal water or by the Stein.

The priory is not known to have been active in state matters, nevertheless it was for All Hallows that parliament enacted in 1380 "that no mere Irishman should be permitted to make his profession in this Priory." In 1539, the priory and its lands, having been acquired by King Henry VIII, were given to the city of Dublin. The gift was in recognition of "the great services, labours, famine, watchings, effusion of blood, cruel wounds, and lamentable slaughter, which the King's faithful subjects in Dublin recently underwent in strenuously and bravely defending the city against the traitorous siege and cruel attacks of Thomas Fitzgerald, his relatives, and accomplices." The city in its turn, encouraged by Archbishop Loftus, presented the site to the crown and in about 1592, Queen Elizabeth I, eulogised as "that Mother of Learning" granted her charter for the establishment of Trinity College. The existing buildings of the priory were demolished, with the exception of a tower at the north-east corner. The first stones of the new college were laid in 1593, and the college opened in 1594.

It is thought that the Hatfield Plan was a proposal for the layout of the college sent to Lord Burghley, first chancellor of the new university, for his consideration, and later generally adopted. It shows the buildings around a single quadrangle with, to the north, the river in a channel between banks of tidal slob. Between the slob and the college are a low wall and a narrow field. In the river a two-masted ship in full sail moves upstream, and the proximity of the college to the river is clear. The plan identifies the north-east tower as "the steeple: a sea marke", and it may be that

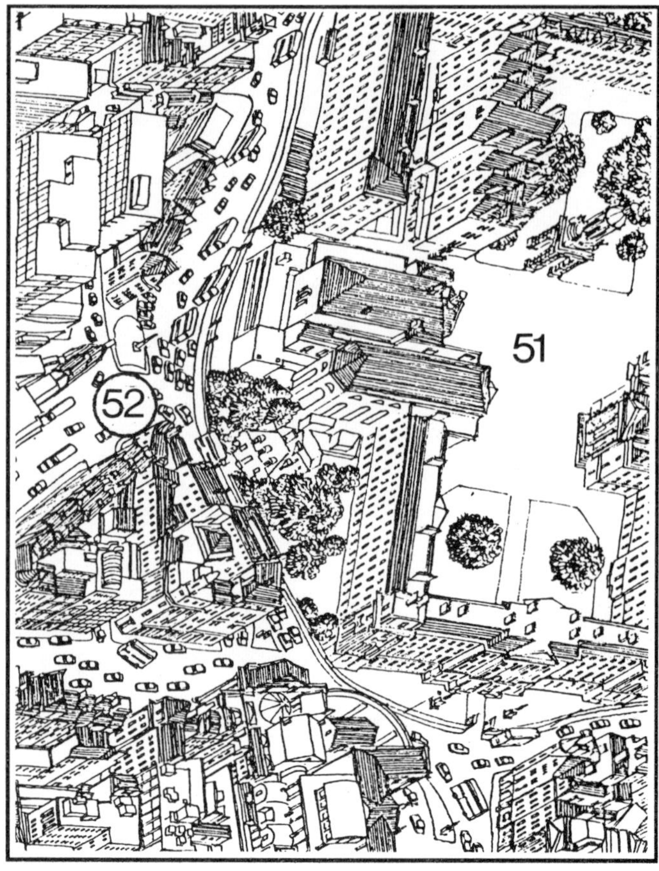

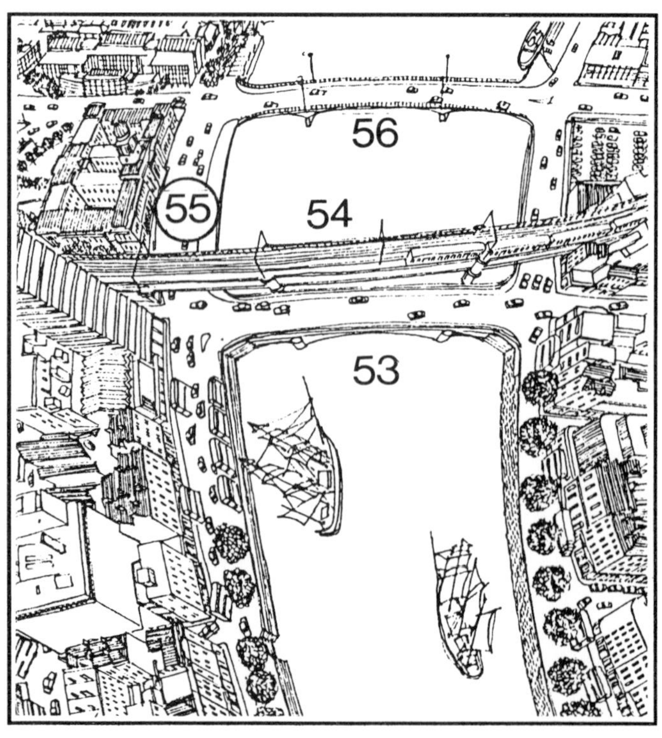

it was the long-standing use of this tower as a navigation mark for vessels entering the port that led to its proposed retention.

Since the building of Hawkins Wall shortly before 1670, Trinity College has generally been protected against direct flooding from the Liffey.

52. THE RIVER STEIN

Also known as the Steine, Steyne, Steyn, Stayne, Stayn, Staine.

This little river, the shortest of the Liffey tributaries in the city rose possibly in Lennox Street or near Harcourt Terrace and flowed towards the southwest corner of Saint Stephen's Green. It then continued under the Royal College of Surgeons and down a line between Grafton Street and Clarendon Street to the corner of Trinity College, flowing past the west face of the college in marshy land and into the Liffey near the junction of D'Olier Street and Hawkins Street.

Due to its location, it figured extensively in the very early history of the city. The shore at its mouth would appear to have been a recognised haven for the Norsemen of the tenth century. It was there that they set up their Long Stone to establish their landing place, perhaps thereby giving both the stream and the meadowland areas stretching out towards Merrion Square and beyond, their name of Stein.

It remained as an open stream for several centuries, being noted as having a timber bridge across it in 1302 and being shown for much of its length by John Speed in his map of 1610. It probably went underground into culverts and pipes in the late seventeenth century as building extended towards Saint Stephen's Green. The tide still continued to back up through the culverts, however, for another two hundred years or so, and it is recorded that a servant was drowned in the nineteenth century in the basement of a house near Grafton Street when water from the stream burst up through the floor and engulfed her.

The Long Stone itself stood about four metres high and survived at least until the end of the seventeenth century, that is for perhaps eight hundred years. It is shown on the Down survey map of 1654 and is referred to in formal documents as late as 1679. It was thrown down probably in the eighteenth century and disappeared. A new pillar has recently been erected in substantially the same position.

53. BUTT BRIDGE

In 1876, royal assent was given to a bill to build a new bridge downstream of O'Connell Bridge. It was made a condition that the bridge should have an opening span to allow ships to lie at Burgh Quay and Eden Quay. A design was prepared for a four-span bridge, containing a fixed masonry approach span at each end with a central iron structure, thirty-eight metres long, that could swing horizontally on the central pier, thus opening two navigation spans each twelve metres wide. The bridge was opened for traffic in 1879. It was named for Isaac Butt (1813-1879), barrister and parliamentarian, and was popularly known as the Swivel Bridge.

The Loopline railway bridge was built downstream of Butt Bridge some ten years later, and the swinging structure became two stationary spans.

This bridge had quite steep gradients and its carriageway was only 5.6 metres wide. Not surprisingly therefore it was quite soon decided that it should be replaced. The debate on the replacement echoed some earlier bridge controversies. This time however, it was not the fear of a new bridge being built downstream at a later date, but rather that such a bridge would be precluded if Butt Bridge were replaced. After many years of argument, the principle of a replacement was accepted in 1929 provided a transporter bridge was built at the same time at Guild Street, a project which never saw the light of day.

The new Butt Bridge was designed by Joseph Mallagh and Pierce Purcell and opened to traffic in 1932. It was the first Liffey bridge in Dublin in which reinforced concrete was used.

An inscription on the bridge in Irish and in English reads as follows:

BUTT BRIDGE
BUILT 1879
REBUILT 1932 BY
THE DUBLIN PORT AND DOCKS BOARD
THE YEAR OF THE 31ST INTERNATIONAL
EUCHARISTIC CONGRESS
CHARLES E MC GLOUGHLIN P.C.
CHAIRMAN
THE RIGHT HON ALFRED BYRNE T.D.
LORD MAYOR
JOSEPH MALLAGH B.E., M.INST. C.E.I.
ENGINEER
GRAY'S FERRO-CONCRETE (IRELAND) LTD
CONTRACTORS

54. LOOPLINE BRIDGE

In 1891, with a view to expediting the passage of British mail through Ireland, and to America, an extension of the Dublin and Kingstown railway line was completed from Westland Row (later Pearse Station) to link up with Amiens Street (later Connolly Station), and through there to Kingsbridge (later Heuston Station) and Broadstone. This required the bridge across the Liffey and the viaduct from the bridge to Connolly, which we see today.

A proposal to build this bridge had been under discussion for several years. In 1883, the Paving and

Lighting Committee of the Corporation had asked that permission be refused. Later it was hoped that the bridge could be located downstream of the Custom House, but as it came to be realised that there would be "unsurmountable difficulties" to this being done, the plea became that the bridge "should be made as convenient and the least objectionable as possible."

55. THE CUSTOM HOUSE

The new Custom House was started in 1781 and substantially completed by 1791. The architect was James Gandon (1743-1823). This was one of the stormiest sagas in the history of building in Dublin, resulting in one of the finest buildings that the city has achieved.

As late as 1774, the City of Dublin had appointed a committee to oppose the building of a new custom house, but the House of Commons accepted the view of the Revenue Commissioners that one was required and sanctioned the work. In 1781, John Claudius Beresford, the revenue commissioner, armed with this permission, asked Gandon to come to Dublin to start work, having discussed the project with him privately in London in 1780.

Because of the opposition which he knew still to exist, Beresford advised Gandon to keep out of sight in Dublin, to live in seclusion; and so one reads in Gandon's own words that being some weeks in Dublin "at last I ventured [out] but at very early hours in the morning to walk over the ground [of the proposed building]." In July 1781 he opened the first foundations. On the following Sunday, egged on by what Gandon described as the Pimlico Parliament "many hundreds of the populace met on the ground. Whiskey and gingerbread were in great demand. It was apprehended that a riot would ensue and that the trenches would be filled up. Such was not the result; on the contrary they amused themselves by swimming in them."

The corporation was not to be defeated. They contended, probably correctly, that part of the ground on which the Custom House was being built was still their property, and they objected to its fencing off by the builders. So in September 1781, with neither prior notice nor government authority "the High Sheriff accompanied by an influential member of the Corporation who subsequently became a conspicuous personage as a military general [Napper Tandy] followed by numerous rabble with adzes, saws, shovels, etc, came in a body to the grounds and levelled that portion of the fence which had been thrown up adjoining the North Wall and River Liffey."

Matters simmered down after this gesture, the legalities were resolved, and Gandon was allowed to get on with his building for some years. He would find it necessary to observe later, however, that "whenever Mr Beresford was absent, every obstacle was thrown in my way to interrupt the progress of the works."

Now, he became faced with a more important problem, the intransigence of the building site itself. The Custom House was being built on land reclaimed from the tidal slob, and the type of foundations he might have used normally would not suffice. For this work, then, he used some timber piles, but for much of it he constructed strong rafts of heavy timber, filled in with a form of lime concrete, and laid down on a bed of cut brushwood. On this he formed his mighty building, reinforcing part of its masonry with iron chains.

In 1786, the formal foundation stone was laid by the lord lieutenant, the Duke of Rutland. By 1791 the Custom House was sufficiently complete to be brought into service together with the "Old Dock" 124 metres long and sixty-three metres wide which now lies under Memorial Road. Work would continue on the Custom House complex well into the nineteenth century, although Gandon severed his connection with the project in about 1808.

The Custom House is possibly the most admired work of architecture in Ireland. The river heads sculptured by Edward Smyth have become well known, and the majesty of the building is clear from James Malton's drawing of 1792. On 25 May 1921, only six weeks before the truce between Ireland and England, the Custom House, as the centre for State Records, was attacked and its contents largely destroyed by fire, together with parts of the building. The fabric has been restored, but not the records.

During the Easter Rising in 1916, the Admiralty boat *Helga* lay for some time in the Liffey opposite the Custom House during its attempt to demolish Liberty Hall by shellfire across the Loopline Bridge.

56. TALBOT MEMORIAL BRIDGE

Memorial Road was established on ground formed by filling in the Old Dock beside the east end of the Custom House. Memorial Road opened on the Custom House Quay and the traffic using it joined the streams converging on Butt Bridge and crossing the Liffey there in both directions. In due course the traffic density became so high that it was found necessary to link Memorial Road to Moss Street and City Quay on the south bank with a new bridge, the Talbot Memorial Bridge, making both it and Butt Bridge one-way arteries.

The new bridge, which has three spans, is the first Liffey Bridge to employ the medium of prestressed concrete. It was completed in 1978, the designers being the company of De Leuw, Chadwick and OhEocha and the builders Ascon Limited.

The name of the bridge commemorates the Venerable Matt Talbot (1856-1925), a Dublin man of heroic sanctity, who worked first in the Dublin Port and Docks Board, then for some years as a casual

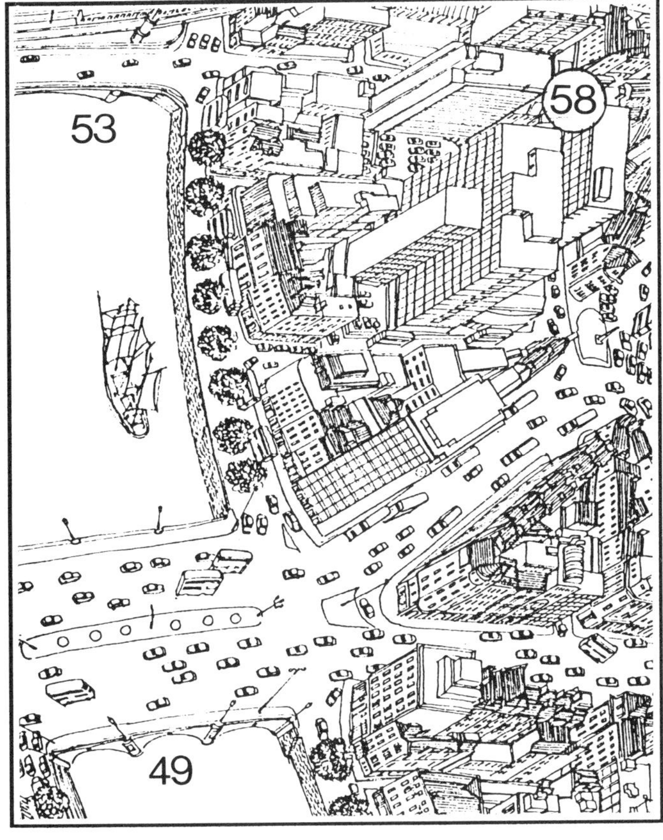

labourer, and for the last twenty-five years of his life in the timber yard of Messrs T and C Martin on the North Wall.

An inscription on a plaque on the bridge in Irish and English reads:

THIS BRIDGE WAS OPENED OFFICIALLY BY
THE RIGHT HONOURABLE THE LORD MAYOR,
COUNCILLOR MICHAEL COLLINS:
14 FEBRUARY 1978

57. THE CUSTOM HOUSE DOCKS

There were three Custom House Dock basins, the Old Dock of 1786, now filled-in under Memorial Road, and George's Dock and the Inner Dock, both planned by John Rennie (1761-1821) in 1821, and built during the following three years. George's Dock, 96 metres by 72 metres, was entered from the Liffey through a lock, and the Inner Dock was then entered by a linking channel, 86 metres long, from George's Dock. A horizontal swing bridge, replaced in 1911 by twinned vertical rolling bridges, preserved the continuity of the North Wall for traffic.

As was appropriate for such large dock basins, extensive new warehouses were built as part of the 1821-1824 scheme. One of these, " the new Tobacco Store", 150 metres long and 48 metres wide, would become publicly known in 1856 when, because it was the only space in Dublin that could sit 3000 people down to dinner, it was used for the banquet that celebrated the end of the Crimean War and the return home of the Royal Dublin Fusiliers.

This complex of docks and warehouses is now to be developed as the site for an international financial services centre.

58. LAZERS HILL

From the beginning of history there was a ridge along the present line of Townsend Street. Imagine all the houses stripped off, from D'Olier Street to beyond Westland Row, and from the south bank of the Liffey to Pearse Street. Now imagine Pearse Street as a very shallow valley, perhaps two to three metres lower than it is today, with the Liffey running parallel to it. Then the shape of what would come to be known as Lazers Hill (a ridge rather than a hill), convex from south to north and horizontal from east to west, can be visualised. At all times the upper slopes of the ridge will be above high-water mark. But on the north side of the ridge the tide will rise and fall on its flank, and on the south, the depression will be damp or waterlogged to some extent all of the time. In the east-west direction, the ridge will be seen to dip slightly into the River Stein while, at its east end, it peters out at Sandwith Street. Indeed, the very

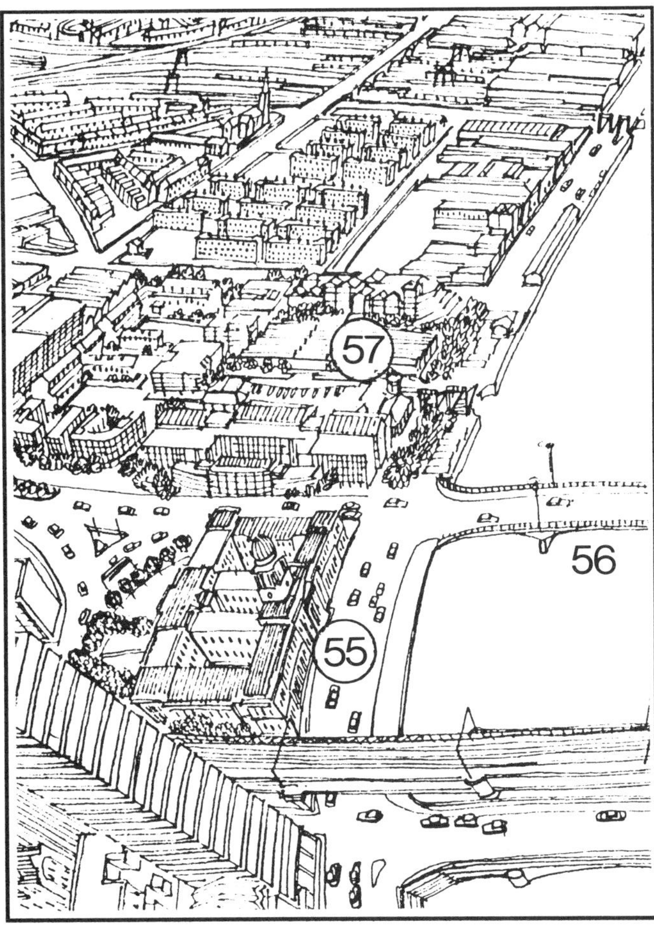

awkwardness of Sandwith Street on a modern map hints at a natural rather than a planned reason for its position: it followed the medieval high-tide shore line.

Lazers Hill probably got its name before or soon after 1215 when Archbishop Henry de Londres built a hospice there for leper pilgrims awaiting passage to the shrine of Saint James of Compostella in Spain. In the following six centuries it would be known as Lazar's Hill, Lazy Hill, Lacy Hill and Lowsie Hill, with many variations. The district was surely lived in from the earliest times. It lay astride one of the routes eastward from Hoggen Green, passing north of the Priory of All Hallows. As the centuries wore on, its population grew, more rapidly probably as its use as a haven for invalid pilgrims declined.

Lazers Hill shared in the upsurge of civil activity in the second half of the seventeenth century. In 1673, the high-tide shore line followed Hawkins Wall and then roughly the line of modern Poolbeg Street and South Gloucester Street before turning south-east to follow Sandwith Street right through to Hogan Place and Grand Canal Street. Pearse Street did not exist. By 1760, that shore line would have been pushed back to Sir John Rogerson's Quay and the modern South Lots Road, although not all the newly contained land would have been properly reclaimed.

Lazers Hill had a population in 1659 of 237 persons, of whom 180 were English and 57 Irish. (Ringsend at the same time had a population of 80.) Lazers Hill presents a wide variety of interests. A forty-year sample suggests this diversity:

1671:   A bridge was proposed from Lazers Hill across the Liffey.
1673:   the frigate "Lambay Catch" was rebuilt and launched.
1676:   The ownership of a public house "The Dun Horse" was in litigation.
1689:   Lazy Hill Walk was supplying 16 horses to the brewery trade.
1702:   It was being proposed that a Mansion House be built in the district for an incoming lord mayor.
1713:   "Guild brethren of the Cutlers, Painter-stainers, and Stationers are ordered to attend the Standard at 6 oclock on the morning of 13th August at Mr Warden Wine's house on Lazy Hill, their hats edged with gold, bearing cockades of red and yellow, and wearing yellow gloves stitched with red silk and bound with red ribbon." They were to take part in the riding of the franchises.

The loss of a sense of district probably began with the building of Great Brunswick Street, now Pearse Street, at the turn of the eighteenth century. In 1756, Pearse Street was a collection of gardens and or-chards merging into the parks of Trinity College. In 1838, it existed as a street fully built-up on both sides, with College Park behind the houses on the south side. The ridge had vanished.

The name of Lazers Hill was still being used on official documents in 1815. By 1838 the street on the former ridge was no longer Lazers Hill but Townsend Street; and the South Lots had been developed to lock Sandwith Street into a system of planned streets. This awkwardly placed street remains now as possibly the sole geographical evidence of the district that for six hundred years was Lazers Hill.

59. THE HIBERNIAN MARINE SCHOOL

(Also known as the Marine Nursery)

In 1760, the Hibernian Marine Society was founded in Dublin to aid the families of seafaring men. In 1766, the society opened a school at Irishtown. It could accommodate about twenty boys from seven to fourteen years of age, and its purpose was to give them a general education and some knowledge of the sea to prepare them to become apprentices to the masters of ships.

In 1768 the society took a site on Sir John Rogerson's Quay, between Cardiff's Lane and Lime Street and in 1773 opened a school there for about 200 boys. In an interesting condition of residence, possibly intended to strengthen in the children the sense of being Dubliners, the pupils were accustomed to "march on Franchises Day."

James Malton attributed the design of the school to Thomas Ivory (1720-1786), but it is suggested by later authorities that it may have been the work of Cooley. A fine view of the building is given by Malton, and his drawing of 1796 should be seen not only for the school but also for the wealth of contemporary river detail that it shows: rafts, a slip, a crane, timber revêtments or fenders on the quay wall, and river traffic, as well as for the Venice-like aspect of the Custom House upstream.

During the nineteenth century, attendance at the school declined, and in 1872 the building was burnt down. The society continued its work, first in Upper

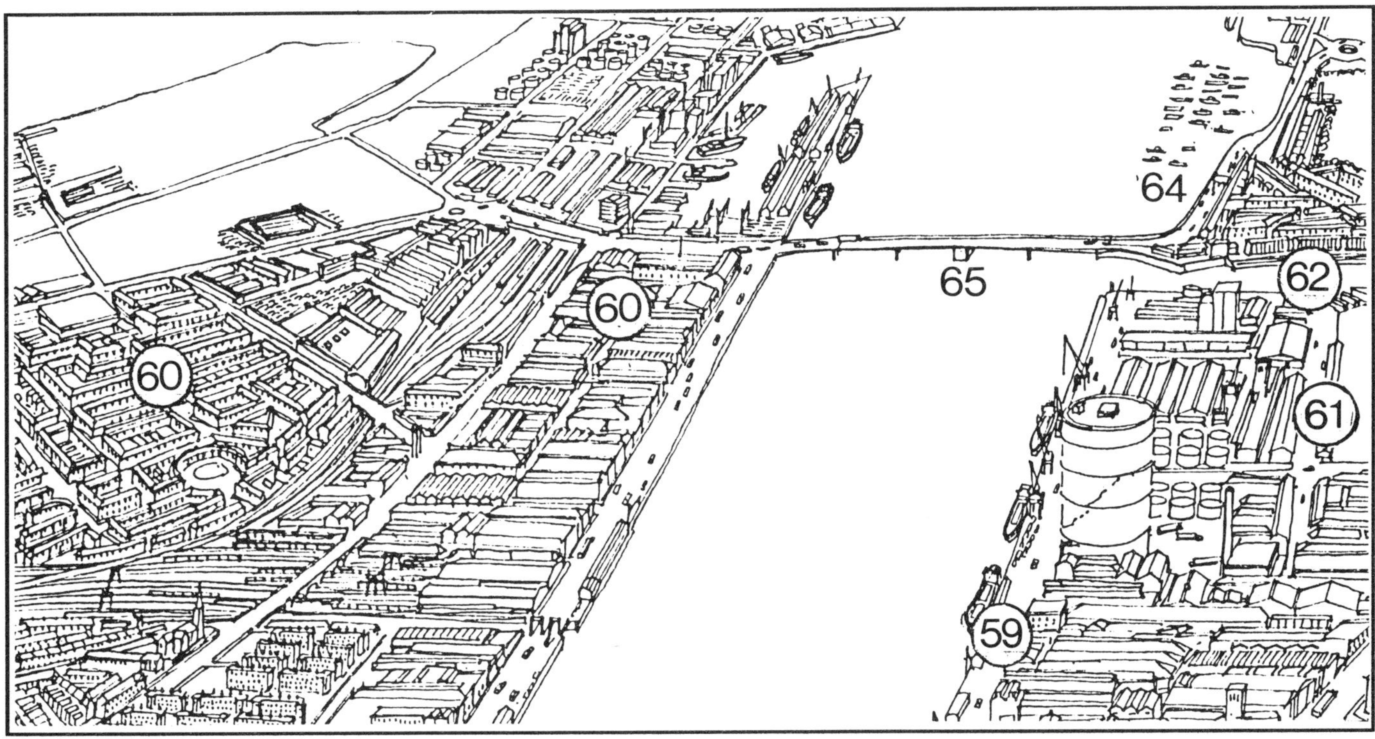

Merrion Street, then in Rathmines, and finally in Clontarf where it is to be found today.

60. THE EAST WALL

A huge exercise in land reclamation was carried out on the north bank of the Liffey in the first thirty years of the eighteenth century. A brief glance at Bernard de Gomme's map of 1673, and John Rocque's map of 1760 or a modern city map, will show its extent. The earlier map shows the high-tide shore line to be more or less straight from Butt Bridge to Ballybough Bridge. By 1730, about two square kilometres of ground had been walled in from the sea in a great quadrangular area reaching from the North Strand out to the north end of the Eastlink Bridge.

The work consisted of building two walls, the North Wall facing the river channel, and the East Wall facing the estuary and the bay. The agency in charge of this project was the Ballast Office, set up in 1707 with a committee of directors appointed by the City Council. They started work on the North Wall in 1710, using a facing wall of wickerwork baskets or kishes, filled with stone, backed by a filling of material dredged from the channel of the river; but this system would gradually be replaced by stone walling. The North Wall had been completed by 1718, and then the East Wall was started and carried along the line of the present East Wall Road up to Ballybough Bridge, now Luke Kelly Bridge (Annesley Bridge came much later, in 1793). The East Wall had been completed by

1728 and Charles Brooking in his map of that year could write "this part is walled in but as yet overflowed by ye tide."

The City Council initiated a scheme for selling plots of the land that was being reclaimed. In 1717, 263 plots ranging in size from three-and-a-half acres to about half an acre were noted by the Council. These were the North Lots, and the map of the allocation, listing the names of the purchasers between Sheriff Street and the North Strand, is in itself an interesting social record of the time.

The building of the East Wall, part of which can still be seen at Annesley Bridge, did not mean instant reclamation. Some of the area was still being filled in the nineteenth century, although by 1838 the Ordnance Survey map showed that only two small parts near the modern Merchants Road and East Road were under water. The work of reclamation had passed in 1786 by an Act of the Irish Parliament from the Ballast Office to the Corporation for Preserving and Improving the Port of Dublin (sometimes known as the Ballast Board), which in turn would hand over to the Dublin Port and Docks Board in 1867.

The area covered by the sale of lots was extensive, reaching up into Fairview. Many whose lots lay north and east of the new channel of the Tolka would have had to wait for the Great Northern Railway embankment and the even later Fairview Park to see their allocations as dry land. Others were more fortunate. The 1838 Ordnance Survey map shows several large residences in the reclaimed area. One of these, Forbes

Castle, is close to a lot allocated to Alderman George Forbes on East Road in 1717. A stone found in the vicinity suggests that the house was built or at least named in 1729.

One result of this reclamation was the obliteration of the entity known as Mud Island. This small area, centred near the modern Charleville Avenue, may well in earlier times have been an island at high tide. It clearly did house its own tightly-knit community, probably over many centuries.

Much of the flourishing East Wall district is today below the level of very high tides in the river; but it is protected by the now generally invisible East Wall, and by the extensive land developments in the port.

61. THE CANAL DOCKS

In 1760 the Grand Canal had reached Dublin and established its city terminus at James's Street Harbour. Twenty-five years later the linking of this harbour to the Port of Dublin was an issue, and a proposal had been offered to make the link by a dizzy ladder of locks straight down through what is now Guinness's brewery to the Liffey. Fortunately there was an alternative proposal to bring the canal around by the Circular Road. In 1791 permission was given for this scheme, provided it included the provision of a riverside dock, and could be completed in four years. The work was successful and, on Saint George's Day in 1796, the Grand Canal Docks were opened near Ringsend, with glittering vice-regal ceremonial, by the Earl of Camden. He sailed into the dock in the yacht *Dorset*, watched by a gathering of 60,000 with flags waving, bands playing, guns booming, and a splendid breakfast in a tent for the lord lieutenant.

This dock contains some twenty-four acres of water and 1800 metres of berthage, and the locks that connect it to the river are near the confluence of the Dodder and the Liffey at Great Britain Quay.

This is not the place to enter into the piquant story of the Royal Canal, rival for the Dublin-Shannon trade. Its link across the north of Dublin, from its city terminus at Broadstone to the Liffey, was made in 1796. It also terminated in a dock, connected to the river through locks. This dock was not at all as pretentious as its competitor across the river, being more a widening of the canal then a distinct dock basin. It was known at first as the Royal Canal Docks. In 1873 however, possibly at the prompting of the Midland Great Western Railway Company and its associates, who were building the North Wall railway station and making a major railway depot nearby, a further part of the already widened canal was developed and formally named for Earl Spencer, the lord lieutenant, as the Spencer Dock.

The nineteenth century was to see the gradual

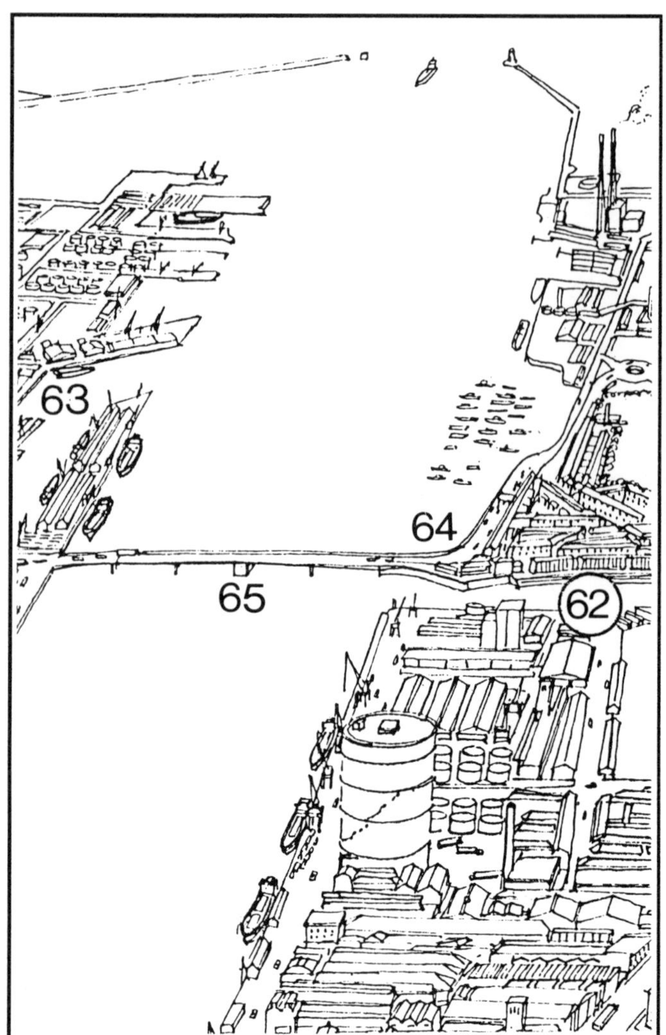

decline of canal traffic in Ireland, and there is regrettably little to add about the later history of the canal docks.

62. THE RIVER DODDER

The River Dodder has also been known as Rathfarnham Water, Dother, Doney River, Donney Brook. It rises on the north side of Kippure Mountain and flows north through Bohernabreena, Rathfarnham, Milltown, Donnybrook, and Ballsbridge to enter the Liffey at Ringsend. It can be a furious and uncontrolled river in spate, as events in 1986 showed. Gerard Boate, writing in the seventeenth century records the drowning in the Dodder below Ballsbridge of "Mr John Usher, father to Sir William Usher that now is, who was carried by the current, no body being able to succour him, although many persons, and of his nearest friends both a-foot and on horseback, were by on both the sides."

In the seventeenth century, the Dodder split into a number of branches to form a delta from Ballsbridge to the Liffey. These flowed at first through meadows liable to occasional inundation and then, on about the line of Bath Avenue, spilled out onto a strand that was covered twice each day by the tide. The west side of this delta was the shore road from Shelbourne Road to Sandwith Street.

The east side was the slightly raised gravelly spit of land with Irishtown at its root and Ringsend at its tip. Like any delta with multiple branches, it was wayward and liable to change its course overnight. This it once did, cutting a new channel and apparently leaving a newly-made bridge high and dry with no water under it.

By 1760, when John Rocque published his general map of Dublin County and Bay, Rogerson's Wall and an embankment along the South Lots Road had blocked all normal tides off from a large part of the delta.

For many centuries the Dodder was a formidable obstacle to travel between Ringsend and Dublin. At low tides in dry periods the journey could be made by fording the river and crossing the strand. But in difficult conditions of tide and weather it was necessary to go around by Irishtown and Ballsbridge, where the bridge was quite frequently impassable anyway. Several attempts were made to bridge the Dodder at Ringsend, beginning in about 1730, but it was not until 1803 that the present bridge at Ringsend Road was completed.

The Dodder was also an added source of difficulty to navigation in the Liffey because of the large quantities of detritus it carried into the channel. For this reason, and possibly to overcome the problem of bridging, it was suggested in 1778 that the entire river should be re-routed through the neck of the peninsula near Saint Matthew's church in Irishtown directly on to the South Bull sands. Had this diversion been made, it is quite possible that Ringsend, becoming technically an island, might have been fortified, as indeed had earlier been proposed, to create a citadel controlling the movement of hostile ships in the bay and river.

63. THE NEW PORT

In a historical sense the new port of Dublin might include everything between the new Custom House and the bay. This note however mentions only what is situated on new ground on the north bank east of the eighteenth-century East Wall. The Canal Docks are discussed in another note.

The earliest work in this area was carried out by the Corporation for Preserving and Improving the Port of Dublin before its function was taken over by the Dublin Port and Docks Board in 1867. The first development was a boat-building and repair yard with a launching slip, known as the Patent Slip. This was in position by 1833 on a site opposite the end of Sheriff Street. This was followed by the port's first dry dock or graving dock completed in 1860, together with the ground reclaimed around it which continues today as a site for boat repairs.

The Port and Docks Board on its inception began a programme of development and during the ensuing thirty years, up to 1894, built a new river quay — the North Wall Extension, or North Quay Extension — and formed behind it possibly its principal work of the nineteenth century, the Alexandra Basin. It was in these works that Bindon Stoney used the precast blocks of concrete, weighing up to 300 tons each and carried into position with a floating hoist, which were to arouse worldwide admiration and interest among engineers.

It was on the North Quay Extension that, in 1905, there was erected the huge 100-ton turret crane that, until 1987, dominated the port skyline; and it was off this quay that the world's largest ship of the time, *The Great Eastern*, 204 metres long, lay during her visit to Dublin in 1886.

There was a lull then in the development of the port until the 1920s when Alexandra Quay was built along the north side of the Alexandra Basin, to be followed by Alexandra Quay East, the Ocean Pier and the oil jetties, all to be completed by about 1955. At this time a major programme of land reclamation, still in progress, had begun, and was pushing the boundaries of the port lands northward along the East Wall and towards the Clontarf shore. And at this time, in 1957, a second graving dock was built, and opened by the President of Ireland Mr Seán T O Kelly.

During the past thirty years industrial enterprises have been set up on the reclaimed land. The timber yards that once dotted the river banks in the old town are now along Bond Road (on top of Clontarf Island) and Tolka Quay. To the north and east the tanks of the oil zone and the stalking transporters of the ferry terminal symbolise the port for the people of Clontarf.

64. RINGSEND

When the first Norsemen swept into the Liffey in 837, they were surely watched from a small cluster of houses near the tip of a gravelly spit that projected far out into the estuary from its southern shore.

Ringsend has been there from the beginning of Dublin. It was the home of fishermen who lived well on herrings, oysters, mussels, cockles, crabs, as well as mullet, which still come upstream to this day to lie in shoals above O'Connell Bridge.

Five hundred years later, the Normans held power over the land of Ringsend, and the gravel spit and its community were part of the estate of Thorncastle. The name of Ringsend had not yet appeared. One of the earliest references to it occurs in the riding of the city franchises in 1488 when the hamlet was named as "the Rynge's ende".

Imagine it then, not more than 200 metres wide, one kilometre long and only two or three metres above high water, with the bay rising and falling on one side and the sometimes roaring waters of the River Dodder on the other. The people living near the point of the spit (An Rinn) were always seafarers; and they needed to be, because a storm-driven high tide could send the water rushing through their back doors and out the front, if indeed it did not take the houses with it in its passage.

Ringsend was a natural landing place, especially because of the treacherous channel of the medieval Liffey, and during the sixteenth century it began to take over from Dalkey as the deep-sea port of Dublin. In 1582, the city authorities started work on a fortified watch-house for their revenue office. De Gomme's map of 1673 shows this watch-house near the tip of the spit, and the village as a single street with houses on both sides stretching south along its spine.

In 1641 it was accepted that "boats drawing more than seven or eight feet of water cannot go nearer Dublin than the Ringsend"; and it was this feature, possibly augmented by military prudence, that prompted Oliver Cromwell to land there, rather than in the city in August 1649. It is reported that, on his landing, he was "heroically entertained with the resounding echoes of the great guns round about the city" as they were discharged in his honour; and he made, at his landing "a most sweet and plausible speech" (albeit a whit strident) in which he promised to devote all his energies to "carrying on the great work against the barbarous and bloodthirsty Irish." About that time there were fifty-nine English and twenty-one Irish recorded as living in Ringsend. Perhaps the shades of their ancestors passed before them as they watched the Lord Protector and his 12,000 troops disembark from their ships around the village during that summer's day.

The eighteenth century was a prosperous period in Ringsend, even if it lost the herrings which left the bay at that time. The village was now a recognised deep-sea landing place. Boat builders, ships chandlers, innkeepers, hackney drivers and shell fishermen all flourished. Dubliners flocked to the South Bull to bathe, and the Great South Wall insulated them all from the worst fury of the sea. By 1803 the isolation of Ringsend from the city had been ended by the final bridging of the Dodder, and the brigand belt of Beggar's Bush had been largely neutralised.

The urbanisation of Ringsend however brought its own maladies. Industries not welcome in the city were established there. The mail packets, like the herrings, left the river and went to Howth and Kingstown, and the commerce associated with the cross-channel traffic and the building of the wall declined. In 1818, a sailor passing up-river to a berth near the Custom House could write of passing "the wretched village of Ringsend consisting of a few ruinous houses with its salt works involved in clouds of black smoke."

Ringsend is still a place of seafarers, a village living vigorously in the suburbs of the city. It still has, and uses, the river; but Cromwell's Steps have been buried in the East Link approaches, the South Wall has little physical meaning, and the sound of the sea breaking on the South Bull has to carry across two kilometres of dry and built-up land if it is to be heard any more in the village.

65. EASTLINK BRIDGE

The building of a road bridge across the Liffey in the docks area was a topic discussed over many years. On one hand was the need to establish a traffic artery from north to south at the east side of the city. On the other was the blocking off of important stretches of the downstream quays to shipping. Bridges of many forms were proposed: low-level bridges; high-level bridges that would require long approach slopes to take them above passing vessels; transporter bridges that would pick up vehicles and carry them across the river in a travelling cradle suspended from a high gantry.

In 1976 the industrialist, Tom Roche, proposed a bridge at the junction of the North Wall Quay and the East Wall Road to cross to the south bank near Ringsend and to connect there to a new road system passing east of the city. This bridge, which was to have an opening span to allow access for shipping up as far as the Loopline Bridge was to be built as a private enterprise and was to be a toll bridge. Approval was given in 1982. The bridge, in reinforced concrete with the 180-tonne opening span in steel, designed by the company of Mc Carthy and Partners and built by

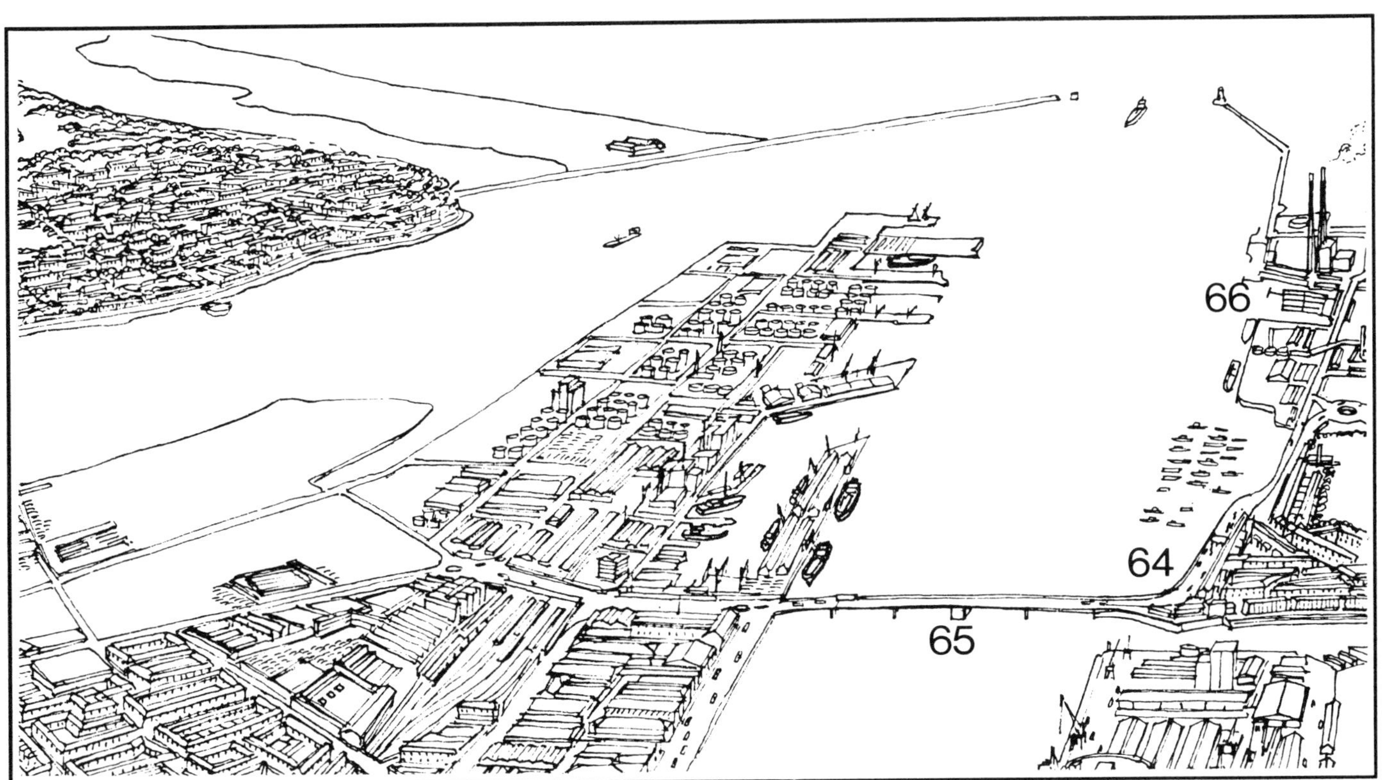
66
64
65

Irishenco Ltd, was formally opened on 21 October 1984. Soon vehicles were crossing the bridge at a rate in excess of 11,000 each day and, by February 1985, over a million vehicles had used this crossing.

A feature of historical interest associated with this project was the building of the approach road from the south in the tideway of the Liffey, on the river side of the Great South Wall. The opening of the bridge was heralded on the previous day by the ending, after more than six hundred years, of the saga of the city's public ferries.

66. THE PIGEONHOUSE

One cannot be terse about the Pigeonhouse. To discuss it, one must consider the Green Patch and also John Pidgeon, The Pidgeon House, Pigeonhouse Harbour, The Tunstalls, Pigeonhouse Hotel, Pigeonhouse Fort, Pigeonhouse Sewage Treatment Plant and the Pigeonhouse Electricity Generating Station.

At the "knuckle" of the Great South Wall, there was, early on, a small area of land that remained dry at high tide and presumably grew grass. On this "green patch" a house had been built to collect and store goods and materials from wrecks. The Ballast Office employed watchmen at this place. In the late eighteenth century, John Pidgeon was a watchman or an overseer, and the house acquired his name as John Pidgeon's House, or perhaps through the humour of his companions, the Pigeonhouse.

In 1755 the causeway had been made from Ringsend to the Green Patch and already in 1775 the whole "knuckle" area had been developed. It now contained three large buildings and a substantial, although never very successful, harbour. The whole was called Pidgeon House on a contemporary map. In 1787, enlarged premises were built by the Ballast Office and these included accommodation for Francis Tunstal, a supervisor, and his wife.

Pigeonhouse Harbour was at this time the cross-channel mail port and had a steady passenger traffic. Some twenty years later a visitor would write: "our vessel was able to lie alongside of the Pigeon-house, where we quitted that consummation of human misery, a cabin after a short voyage." Not surprisingly, there appeared quite soon to be an opening for a hotel at the harbour, and in 1790 Mrs Tunstal was in charge of the new Pigeonhouse Hotel. Some idea of its nature may be gained from a contemporary list of part of its contents.

2 mountain stone chimney pieces,
14 black stone chimney pieces,
9 Kilkenny marble chimney pieces with hearths,
1 large Tuscan "fronticepiece" with cornice etc.
A moulded architrave and arch over the hall door.

The hotel would give good service to voyagers until

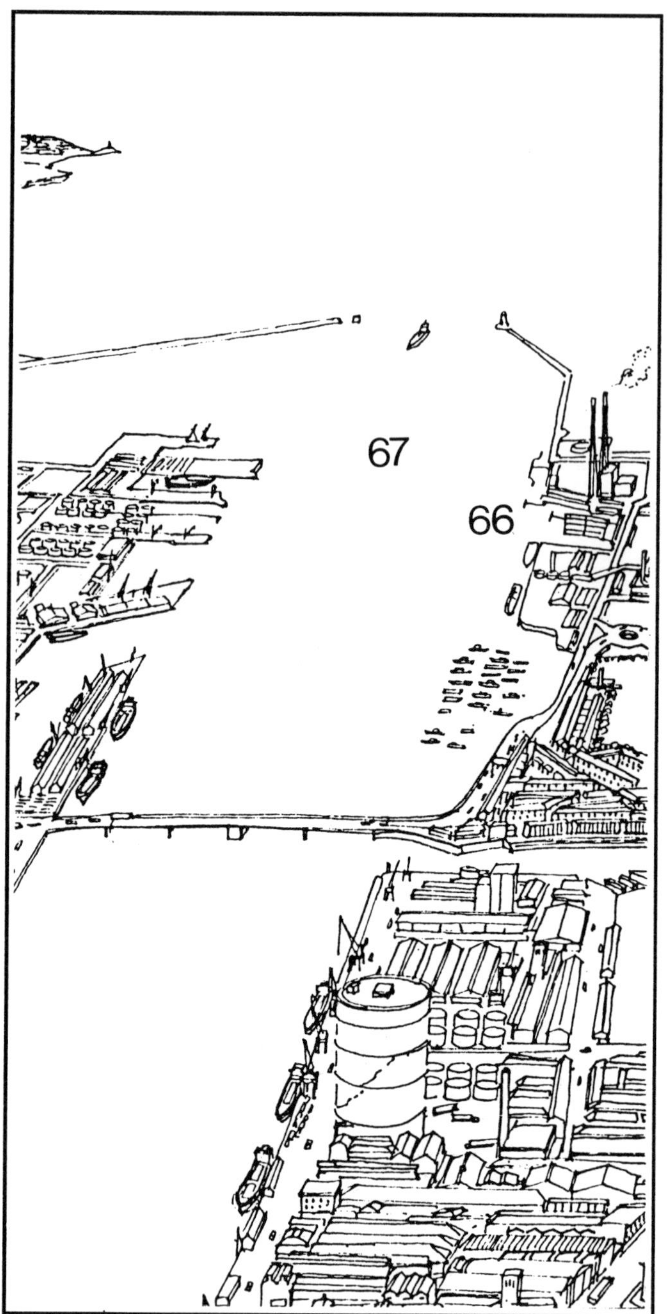

Howth harbour took over the cross-channel mail and passenger traffic around 1810. Afterwards, it would continue to be, like the Conniving House in Irishtown, a place of solace to Dubliners in need of a convivial dinner; and this would continue until the time of the Young Ireland movement of 1848 when Pigeonhouse Fort would become exclusively military and the hotel would be closed.

At the time of the rebellion of the United Irishmen in 1798, the British government had established a stockaded military fort at the Pigeonhouse, and in 1813, probably after the winding-down of the harbour as a cross-channel terminal, they purchased the area outright from the Ballast Board. The Pigeonhouse Fort was gradually strengthened until in 1835 it could be shown on a contemporary map as an extensive complex of buildings stretching for over 300 metres along the south and east of the harbour. The Pigeonhouse Fort remained as a stronghold right through the nineteenth century until 1897 when it was sold back to the city.

The use of the area then changed radically. In the years from 1896 to 1906, Dublin built a comprehensive sewerage system for a large part of the city, and the Pigeonhouse harbour was converted into a series of settlement tanks as part of the system. At about the same time, in 1903, Dublin's infant electricity undertaking, becoming too big for its accommodation in Fleet Street, moved out to establish at the Pigeonhouse the first in a series of generating stations. The foundation stone for the new works had been laid by the Lord Mayor, Timothy Harrington, M.P. in 1902. The old name would be retained by the Electricity Supply Board for some decades, but the latest station on the site has been given the name of Poolbeg.

The remains of the fortifications may still be seen, and the spaciousness of the former harbour observed. The area has remained known to the people of Dublin, as it is on the route to the Great South Wall. The establishment during the last decade of a new sewage treatment plant in reclaimed ground some little way to the south might make possible at some time in the future the recovery of the harbour basin and reveal yet another new role for the basin and the courtyards of the fort. The final chapter of the history of the Pigeonhouse has perhaps not yet been written.

67. THE POOLS IN THE ESTUARY

The naturalist Gerard Boate, writing in about 1641, described Dublin as a lesser or inferior haven because of the sandbank or bar at the mouth of the Liffey and the open storm-prone expanse of Dublin Bay. He described the river mouth for mariners: "This haven almost all over falleth dry with the ebbe, as well below Rings-end as above it, so as you may go dry foot round about the ships which lye at an anchor there, except in two places, one at the north side, half way

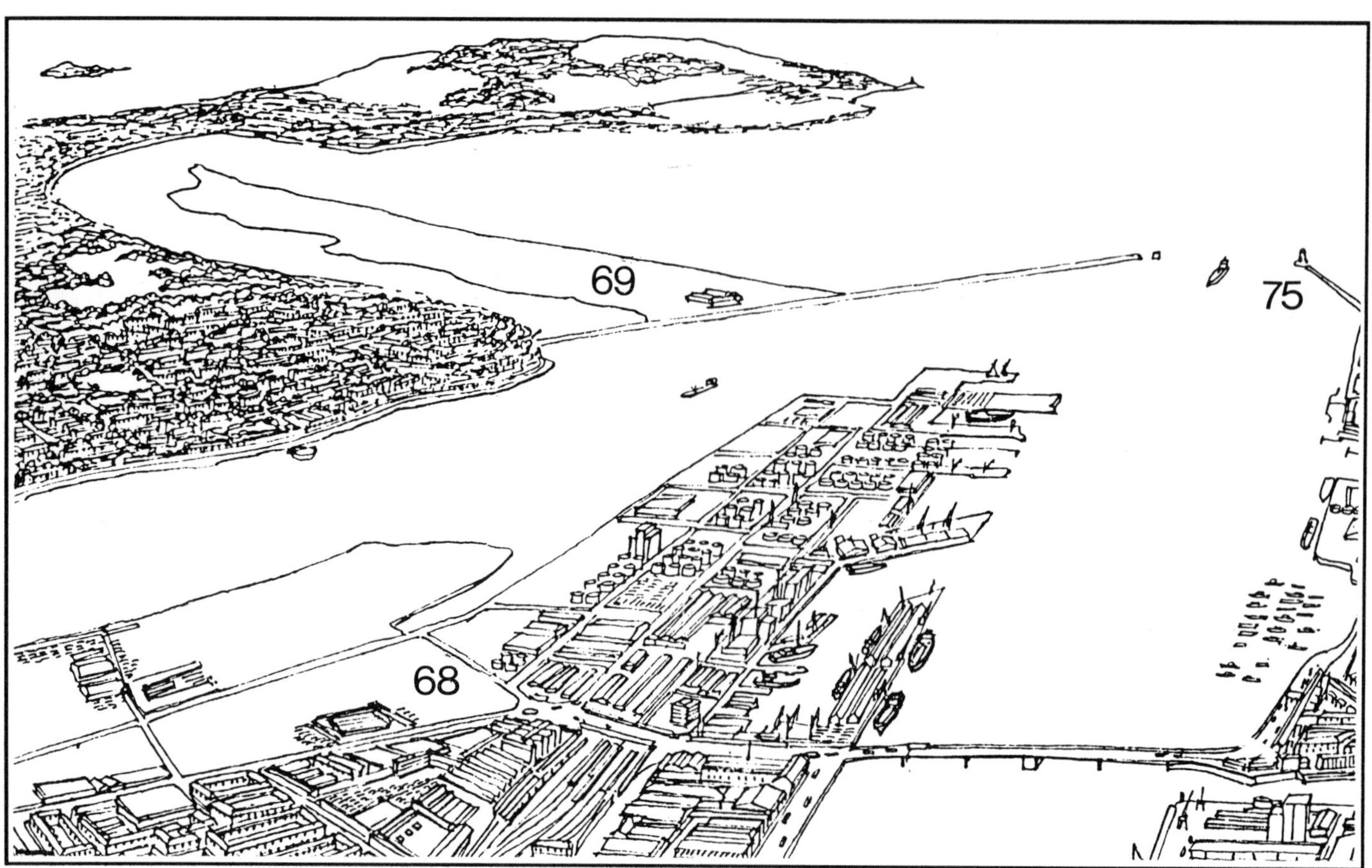

betwixt Dublin and the bar, and the other at the south side not far from it. In these two little creeks (whereof the one is called the pool of Clontarf and the other Poolbeg) it never falleth dry but the ships which ride at an Anchor remain ever afloat; because at low water you have nine or ten feet of water there."

Others have in fact shown four pools in the estuary of the river, the two named, and also the Salmon Pool and the Iron Pool. Using modern landmarks, the Iron Pool lay from the seaward side of Poolbeg lighthouse upstream as far as the Half Moon Battery on the Great South Wall; Poolbeg upstream from there nearly to the Poolbeg electricity generating station; the Salmon Pool upstream from there to the entrance to the Alexandra Basin a little below Ringsend; and the Pool of Clontarf to the north of the Salmon Pool and somewhat off the main channel of the Liffey.

While these pools did allow ships to remain afloat at all tides, and did as a result become crowded, they gave no protection against the fury of the wind. Thus in 1609 the *William of Aier* turned turtle in Poolbeg during a storm, while twenty years earlier, John Forster and Skipper Berns had been enjoined to "remove the carcas of their ould hulke which perished in the pole of Clontarf "and had been warned that "yf they fayle therin, that Mr Mayor shall comytt theire boddies unto pryson untyll they performe this order."

With the construction of the South Wall and Bull Wall, and to some degree the East Wall, the significance of the pools diminished. The whole area tended to be known as Poolbeg, and reference to pools in the Liffey largely ceased.

68. CLONTARF ISLAND

At the sharp bend in East Wall Road, two newer roads, Tolka Quay and Bond Road, branch off to the east and north-east. If one walks about 200 metres along Bond Road, one is now standing on the site of what was, for a thousand years or more, Clontarf Island. Men stood on the island in 1014 during the battle of Clontarf and may perhaps have fled away afterwards in boats beached on its shore.

The island would apparently have been accessible to men on horseback at low tide and it features in the riding of the franchises of the city in 1603. Part of the route then lay "from the furlonge [of Clontarf] to the Island of Clontarfe and so by the river of Anliffe alongst westward" to Saint Mary's Abbey. It was substantially a bank of sand and gravel, perhaps 450 metres long from west to east and 120 metres wide at its widest. Its precise outline was understandably uncertain and it is shown in many different shapes on early maps.

In 1665 when London was stricken with the Great

Plague, the lord-deputy and his Council were concerned about "the great perill and danger which might ensue to this citty of Dublin" due to "the infection of the plague in the citty of London" if persons "of all sorts should be suffered freely to resort hither without controul." Accordingly they ordered that two houses convenient for storing merchandise "and for receaving and entertaining of passengers, and such other persons as shall come from beyond seas, be forthwith erected a convenient distance from this citty." It was agreed "that the island of Clontarffe be appointed as the most convenient place." In 1666, the houses, by then described as the "pesthouses", had been built.

During the eighteenth century, the course of the River Tolka, that had previously flowed to the north and east of Clontarf Island was diverted by coastal works to pass on its west and south. This new course would persist until the virtual disappearance of the island in the nineteenth century and the further realignment of the Tolka.

That the island was gradually being whittled away by man and the elements is clear. Captain Bligh's map of 1800, shows it significantly smaller than it had appeared on earlier maps; and this erosion continued in the nineteenth century with the use of the island as a source for gravel for concrete and also as a source for a shelly sand used as a garden fertiliser.

From 1700 onwards, Clontarf Island, then sometimes called the Bathing Island, was a place of recreation for Dubliners. Ferry boats took them out from a wharf on East Wall Road. They knew this wharf, itself used as a swimming place, as the Smoothing Iron. As late as perhaps 1912, the mitching schoolboys in James Joyce's story "The Encounter" would loiter there during their odyssey, although there was then little of the island left to be seen except at low tide.

Early in the nineteenth century, Christopher Cromwell, a Dublin publican, owned a house on Clontarf Island that he used for fishing. The island had by then, however, become very vulnerable to weather and wave action. In October 1844, during one of the most violent storms ever experienced in the port, its history finally came to an end. It is recorded that at ten o'clock on the night of the storm, the constable on duty in East Wall station saw the light go out in Cromwell's house. The following morning, most of the house and much of what had remained of the island had been washed away. Sadly, Christopher Cromwell and his son William had been drowned.

69. THE NORTH BULL AND BULL ISLAND

Prior to 1700, the low-tide shore line on the north of the river followed a wandering course from Sutton to the present site of O'Connell Bridge. This shore line of sand and shingle was broken three times, by the channel of the River Tolka, and by the two ends of Sutton Creek where it left and rejoined the main waters of the bay. Sutton Creek generally followed the high water shore line of today, through Kilbarrack along Dublin Road, James Larkin Road at St Anne's Park, and Clontarf Road past Dollymount, turning south near the Sheds of Clontarf to rejoin the river. The area of sands contained by Sutton Creek and the low-water shore line of the Liffey estuary was usually shown on the early maps as the North Bull. At high tide the whole area would be covered with water, while at low tide it was a prodigious source of cockles and other shellfish. Names like Crab Lake, Cockle Point and Cockle Hall, given to landmarks along the Clontarf shore by Captain William Bligh in his survey of 1800, underline this trade. The areas known as Bull Wall and Bull Island were therefore part of the North Bull as described.

The North Bull sands were closely associated with the sandbank that formed the bar of Dublin. The bar gravely hindered the use of the port of Dublin and many ingenious attempts were made to circumvent it. One scheme offered by Captain John Perry in 1725 was for a harbour at Sutton to give access to a channel to be formed by deepening Sutton Creek through which ships could make their way along the north shore to sail out into the river proper near Ringsend. Thomas Rogers of Howth would develop this idea in 1800, proposing a harbour at Howth and a canal cutting through the isthmus at Sutton to follow the channel proposed by Perry.

Neither plan was adopted and it was not until the Great South Wall was built and, more significantly, until 1820-1825 with the building of the Bull Wall, that a major improvement was made in the channel for shipping at the bar. This improvement arose, broadly speaking, from the transfer by tidal currents of sands that had formerly tended to build up at the bar over to an area north-east of the Bull Wall, an area which then gradually grew to be the island known today as North Bull Island, or simply the Bull Island. It is interesting to note that the Bull Island that is now four kilometres long and contains two golf links, a bird sanctuary, and strands which are extensive at all stages of the tide, grew from the small oval sandbank about 150 metres long and fifty metres wide that Captain Bligh surveyed in 1800.

The timber bridge known as the Bull Bridge was first built in 1819-1820 by R Bergan and Company, and the causeway that finally blocked the flow through Sutton Creek was made in 1964-1965. The last vessel to be wrecked in Dublin Bay, the Wexford schooner *Antelope*, was driven aground on the shore of Bull Island in December 1950 and parts of the wreckage were still to be seen quite recently.

The name "Bull" has been suggested as originating in the roar of the surf breaking across the sands. If this is correct, one may then speculate whether this name was given by English-speaking mariners in

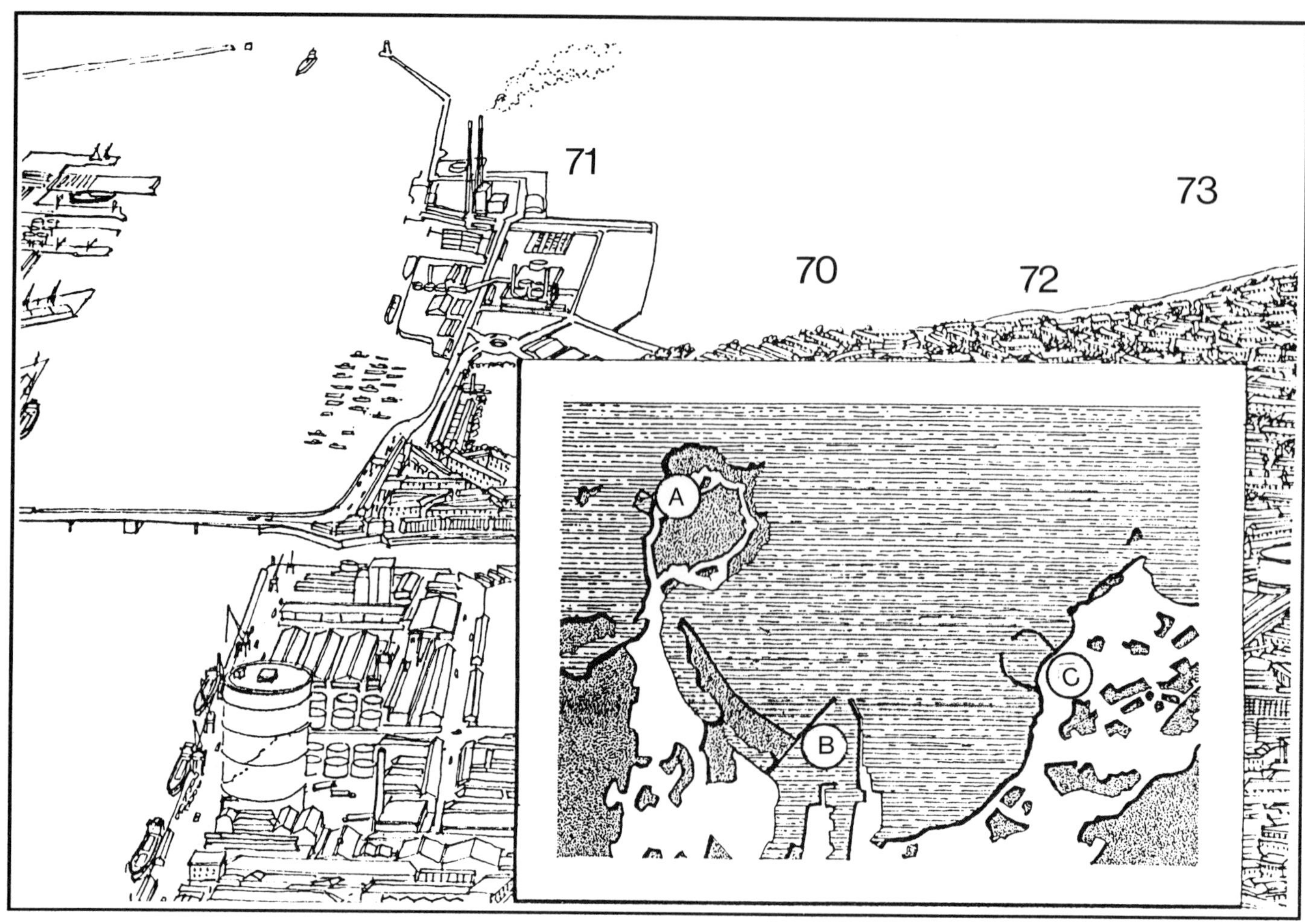

Detail shows Dublin Bay and A: Howth Head B: Estuary of the Liffey and C: Dunlaoghaire

Norman times or later, or whether there is a direct link between its use and the Irish word *tarbh*, as in Clontarf (Cluain Tairbh: "the meadow of the bull"), a name known in the tenth century.

70. THE SOUTH BULL

The area known as the South Bull was a great triangle of sand with its apexes at Ringsend, near the present Poolbeg lighthouse, and at Dunlaoghaire. In the course of the eighteenth century, the north edge of the South Bull was defined precisely by the building of the Great South Wall. The south boundary up to the nineteenth century ran past the side of Irishtown, along a shoreline marked possibly by a bank of shingle to the present Merrion Gates, along the line of Rock Road through Booterstown to Blackrock and then along the rocky shore to Dunlaoghaire. During the nineteenth century the Dublin and Kingstown Railway changed the Booterstown shore line, and the shore from there to Irishtown was made more definite by the formation of Strand Road and its link to Irishtown.

During this present century the corner of the triangle near Ringsend has gradually been reclaimed so that Irishtown, whose strand was famous for bathing in the two previous centuries, has become an inland community and the thousand-year peninsular village of Ringsend has lost its direct contact with the bay and the open sea. The eastern edge of the triangle at low tide, a long sweeping curve of sand from near the Poolbeg to Dunlaoghaire has changed relatively little during the life of the city.

The South Bull, somewhat more accessible to the city than the North Bull and offering an equally lavish supply of shellfish, was an important source of food, employment, and entertainment for Dubliners, and as such has always been jealously guarded as part of the city territory. The sands were seamed with creeks and rivulets, the largest being the Cock Lake channel which followed a curving course from the middle of the eastern edge to the vicinity of the Sandymount Martello Tower, then swinging north to enter the river just below Ringsend. This channel, which also drained a large marsh to the south-east of Sandymount, was sufficiently large to be used by small fishing boats making their way back from the bay to

Ringsend in times of storm. The building of the South Wall and the nineteenth-century reclamation near Sandymount effectively eliminated the Cock Lake channel.

The juxtaposition of the South Bull strand and Irishtown appears in an account of Robert Emmet's planning for the rising of 1803. Emmet's associate at Irishtown was a timber merchant named Thomas Brangan. Richard Madden records, regarding the proposed attack on the Pigeonhouse Fort, which was one of the three main targets, that "Robert Emmet was frequently at Brangan's and on several occasions they walked across the strand when the tide was out to take plans of the Pigeon House and make observations." A hundred years later, Stephen Daedalus would sit on the rocks to contemplate nature, near where Emmet had walked; and later again a memorial would be raised to Joyce to commemorate that part of *Ulysses*.

The South Bull has featured in several episodes of Dublin history and some of these will be found described elsewhere in these notes.

71. THE EASTERN FRANCHISES

Early in the life of Dublin, since the making of accurate maps had not yet begun, it was necessary for the citizens to make a periodic formal tour of the boundaries of their territory so as to establish them, both in their own minds and in the minds of others who might attempt encroachment. In 1200, King John, Lord of Ireland, told his citizens of Dublin what the boundaries of their area of franchise were.

A full description is available of the riding of the franchises in 1488. The part that deals with the south-east corner of the city reads as follows:

"In primis: the said Mayr [Thomas Meyler] and his breethrne tooke ther way, in the name of God, first, owte of the Dameys Gate, and soe forth by the long stone of the Stayn levyng All Hallows on ther right hand, and soe by Ampnlyffy is side tyll they came to the Rynge's ende, and from that to Clar Rade, in Englysh the clere rode for shippes which is now called Polebegge; and from that to Reinelan, now called the barfote, and so estward uppon the Strone on the South side, as fer as a man might ride, and keste a spere into the sea; and then a yeman named William Walsh rode into the watyr and keste a spere into the see at lowe watyr as far as he moghte, and so fer extendeth the fraunches of the seid cittie estward in both the sides of the watyr. And then they rydde bakward till thei came to the blak stone be Este Myrrionge."

The sense is clear. Ringsend was already a fishing village on the end of a gravelly spit at the mouth of the Dodder. The clear road was the low-tide Liffey channel for shipping, and the Reinelan or "point of the island" was the easternmost tip of the South Bull

sands at low water of spring tide. This was perhaps somewhere near the Half Moon Battery on the South Wall. The precise limit of the city boundary was then decided by the lustily-exhorted strength of a yeoman's arm in casting a spear; and this point was accepted for both sides of the river channel. The party, some hundreds strong and mostly on horseback, with banners waving, would then move in procession along the edge of the water across the South Bull in a great arc to Blackrock.

The full round of the city, which took a long summer or autumn day, brought the party down to the river again at Kilmehanoc ford at the western extremity of the franchised territory, and hours later to the mouth of the Tolka, and so home. The riding of the franchises continued for six hundred years into the nineteenth century, the circuit developing as time went on. The custom died out then, probably with the advent of the Ordnance Survey maps in 1838, which made it no longer necessary.

72. THE DRAUGHT OF TURLEYHYDES

In June 1331, a great shoal of very large fish was stranded on the South Bull. It was said that they were so large that two men standing one on each side of a fish could not see one another. There was a shortage of food in Dublin at the time and the lord justice, Sir Anthony Lucy, gave permission to the citizens to slaughter the fish and take away as much as they wished. In the words of James Joyce "a school of turlehide whales stranded in hot noon, spouting, hobbling in the shallows. Then from the starving cagework city, a horde of jerkined dwarfs, my people, with flayers' knives running, scaling, hacking in green blubbery whale meat."

Since it may be thought that this is all Gulliver-like fantasy, it should be mentioned that in 1598 Hendrik Goltzius drew a similar scene showing a sperm whale that had been stranded on a beach at Scheveningen on the Dutch coast. People are shown climbing on the carcass of the whale, and tall men standing by and men on horseback are shown, all dwarfed by its bulk. Indeed, in 1983, a similar stranding of a whale occurred at Bunmahon in County Waterford.

73. THE WRECK OF THE PRINCE OF WALES AND THE ROCHDALE

During the afternoon of Wednesday 18 November 1807, two packet boats, the *Prince of Wales* and the *Rochdale*, sailed out of the Pigeonhouse harbour, as part of a flotilla of ships taking Irish soldiers, accompanied by their families, away to foreign service. That night in the Irish Sea, they ran into a violent storm of wind and snow, which persisted with such intensity during the next day that the captains decided to return to Dublin. They arrived in the bay as night was falling. Being uncertain of their position, and because of the fierceness of the storm, the ships were swept past the small harbour of Dunlaoghaire and were wrecked on the South Bull sands, the *Prince of Wales* under Blackrock and the *Rochdale* near the Martello Tower at Seapoint. Three hundred and eighty people lost their lives, and this in places where they might have waded ashore had they realised the nature of the ground and had the waters been quieter. For several days, their bodies were washed up along the sands between Seapoint and Irishtown.

Many of the victims were buried in the graveyard on the shore at Booterstown where a headstone was erected to their memory. The inscription on the stone reads as follows: "Sacred to the memory of the Soldiers belonging to his Majesty's 18th Regement of Foot and a bevy belonging to other Corps who Actuated by a desire of more Extensive Service Nobly Volunteered from the South Mayo and different Regements of Irish Militia into the line and who were unfortunately Shipwrecked on this Coast in the Prince·of Wales Packet and Perished on the night of the 19th of November 1807 this Tribute to their Memory has been placed on their Tomb by order of GENERAL the EARL of HARRINGTON Commander of the Forces in Ireland."

74. THE GREAT SOUTH WALL

One of the defects of Dublin as a harbour for some nine hundred years was the exposure of the bay and the river estuary to storm. Gerard Boate wrote in about 1641: "the ships have hardly any shelter there from any winds, not only such as come out of the sea, but also those which come off from the land, especially out of the south-west; so as with a great south-west storm the ships run great hazards to be carried away from their anchors and driven into the sea; which more than once has come to pass and particularly in the beginning of November, An. 1637, when in one night ten or twelve barks had that misfortune befaln them, of the most part whereof never no news hath been heard since."

In 1715, the Ballast Office, an agency of the City Council, embarked on what would possibly be the greatest achievement of its eighty years of service. It recorded in that year "it is the opinion of merchants and other skilful men that the south side of the channel, below Ringsend, be piled, which will raise the south bank so high that in time it will be a great shelter for shipping which lye in the harbour."

The project was for a breakwater from Ringsend out to a point in the bay close to the bar, a distance of over five kilometres. Today we see only about two kilometres of wall with water on both sides of it. Until the middle of the nineteenth century, there was a causeway or a wall, with a "knuckle" at the Pigeon-

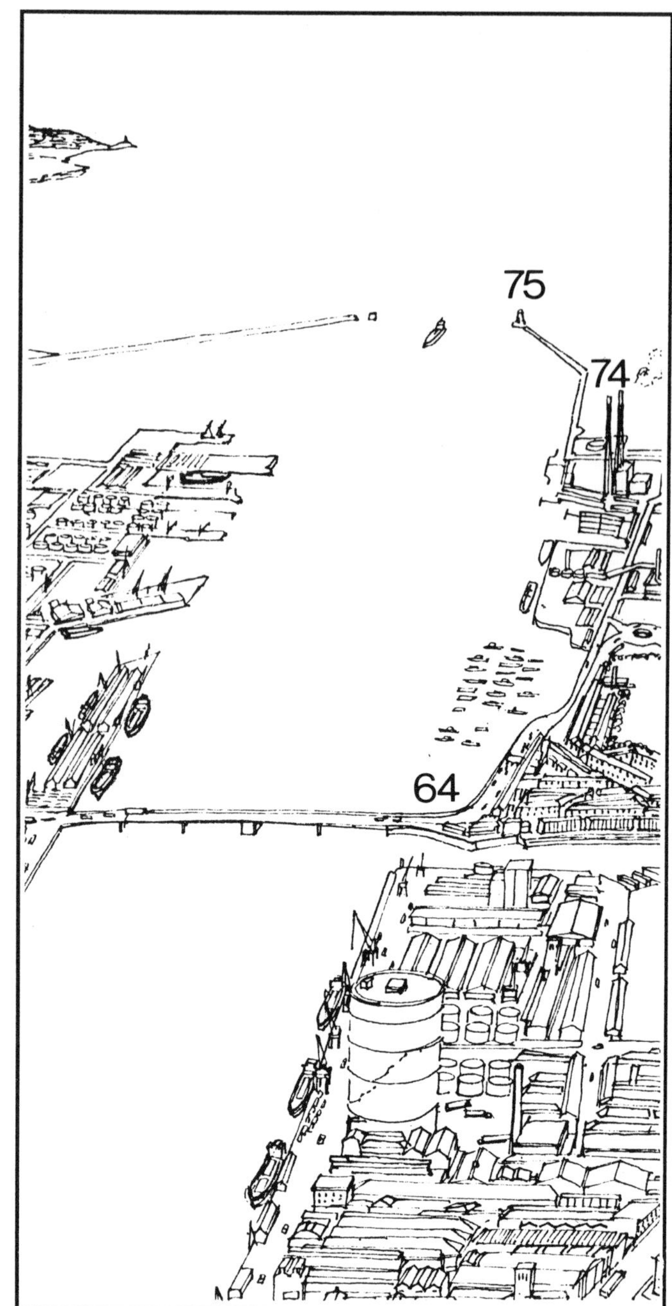

house, with water on both sides all the way from Ringsend to the Poolbeg lighthouse.

The Ballast Office believed that a permanent breakwater could be made with three rows of timber piles or corresponding timber frames filled-in with stones; and they began their work with a pile-driver imported from Holland. Timber — oak and fir — was purchased from Poland, Wales and Sweden to supplement Irish supplies. Some idea of the scale of the work may be gained from the fact that 567 piles were driven in in three summer months of 1717, using the Dutch "engine" and a second pile-driver made in Dublin. By about 1736, a piled or framed breakwater had been extended roughly to the position of the Poolbeg lighthouse.

Quite early in the project, it had begun to be recognised that the timber piling, some of the stumps of which can still be seen at low water, could not resist the winter storms. For many years the Office struggled to keep the breakwater in repair, but twelve years after its completion, they accepted that a stone breakwater was necessary. As a result, in 1748 it was reported that a start had been made to build a stone sea wall back towards Ringsend from about the Pigeonhouse. This part of the wall, which was finished in 1759, would become a causeway with a road serving the Pigeonhouse and parapet walls on both sides. William Sadler's painting of the Pigeonhouse, which shows this in graphic detail, complete with red-coated soldiers and a variety of citizens, is in the collection of the National Gallery of Ireland.

In 1761 the protection of the "head of the piles" out in the middle of the bay with an artificial island of stone was begun. This island was soon converted into the foundation for the Poolbeg lighthouse which was built in the period from 1763 to 1767. At the same time, the construction of a stone wall to replace the frames and piles was started at the lighthouse. Using stone from Clontarf, Blackrock, Bullock and the Dublin Mountains, this wall would gradually be built westward until, about 1795, the entire breakwater from the lighthouse to Ringsend was in stone. The final ten years of this work were under the control of the Corporation for Preserving and Improving the Port of Dublin who, under an Act of the Irish Parliament, had taken over from the Ballast Office in 1786.

In 1801, Captain William Bligh, well-known in naval history as a hydrographer and as the former captain of the South Seas research vessel *HMS Bounty*, advised that the South Wall needed attention from the lighthouse to the Battery (presumably the Half Moon gun emplacement on the Wall) a distance of about one kilometre. By 1818 that part of the wall had been increased in height. Bligh's observation and the reaction to it, both point to the unending struggle needed to maintain the Great South Wall against the violence of the sea, and show clearly how important it has been in the service of the port.

75. THE POOLBEG LIGHTHOUSE

The idea of a lighthouse in Dublin Bay to mark the entrance to the river has a long history. Queen Elizabeth I, in the early years of the seventeenth century, considered a proposal to build a tower similar to the Maiden Tower, established during her reign at Mornington near the mouth of the Boyne. Other proposals were made towards the end of the century.

The idea became a reality however only with the building of an artificial island of stones in 1761 to protect "the head of the piles" later the end of the Great South Wall. In 1762 it was suggested that the island could form the foundation for a lighthouse "if one is found desirable." In 1763, the construction of the Poolbeg lighthouse in stone began, under the supervision of its designer, John Smith. In 1767 the Ballast Office was able to report: "we have advertised in the London, Dublin and Amsterdam Gazettes that there will be a light thereon on the 29th September next"; and they met that date. In 1776, fears were expressed about the safety of the foundations of the structure in heavy seas. During the following three years, an enlarged apron of mountain stone fastened with cast iron was formed around the base of the tower. A hundred years later, in about 1870, this apron was increased in size and strengthened with a ring of huge precast concrete blocks, again bound with iron bands. These various works may be seen today at low water.

Illustrations of the lighthouse, also known as the Cassoon and the George Dublin Lighthouse may suggest a change in its shape since 1767, almost to the point of total reconstruction. Artistic licence must play some part here, as the basic structure was never altered. In 1813, however, there were alterations to the balcony and the access to it, and the overall height of the tower was increased.

The original source of light was from candles. This was changed to oil in 1786, later to petroleum vapour, and finally to electricity generated at the lighthouse. Poolbeg had a resident keeper until 1964. It is now controlled automatically from the Baily lighthouse.

It is at this place, on a line between the Poolbeg lighthouse and the North Bull lighthouse, that the River Liffey ends its journey from Kippure to the sea. It is here, to quote the *Post Chaise Companion* of 1805, that the river "disembogues itself into the ocean"; and perhaps it is here that one may most fittingly leave it.

INDEX

(p) = Illustration

Abbey Quay, 31
Albert Quay, 16
Alen, Archbishop, 32
Alexandra, Queen, 7-8
Alexandra Basin, 49, 54
Alexandra Quay, 16, 49
All Hallows Priory, 37, 38,
   42-3, 46
Amiens Street, 11
Amiens Street Station
   see Connolly Station
Annesley Bridge, 47
Antelope (ship), 55
Archer, William Henry, 35
Aron's Bridge, 23
Arran Bridge, 23
Arran Quay, 16, 24
Arrouaisa, Order of, 42
Art O'Neill's Grave, 6
Artane, 32
Ascon Ltd, 44
Askulv, 38-9
Association for the
   Suppression of Mendicancy
   in Dublin, 22
Aston, Henry, 41
Aston Quay, 16
Ath Cliath, 11-12, 23-4
Athgarvan, 7

Bachelors Lane, 20
Bachelors Walk, 16, 39
Back Quay, 16
Bagnio Ferry, 36
Bagnio Slip, 19, 20, 39
Baily lighthouse, 59
Ballast Board, 47, 53
Ballast Office, 20, 36, 47, 52,
   58-9
Ballsbridge, 49
Ballybough, 31
Ballybough Bridge, 11, 47
Bank of Ireland, 36, 37, 41-2
Barber Institute of Fine Arts,
   36
Barrack Bridge, 20
Barrack Street, 19
Bath Avenue, 49
Bathing Island, 55
Beach Road, 11
Bedford Row, 16, 19
Beggar's Bush, 50
Benburb Street, 11, 18
Benedictine Order, 31
Benson Street, 20
Beresford, John, 40
Beresford, John Claudius, 36,
   44
Bergan, R and Co, 55
Berns, Skipper, 54
Black Pool, 32
Blackhorse Bridge, 15
Blackrock, 56, 59
Blessington reservoir, 6
Bligh, Captain William, 55, 59

Bligh's Map of Dublin, 55

Blind Gate, 37
Blind Quay, 16, 29
Bloody Bridge, 20, 23, 33
Bluebell, 15
Boate, Gerard, 49, 53-4, 58
Bodenstown, Co Kildare, 8
Bohernabreena, 49
Bond Road, 50, 54
Bonham Street, 23
Booterstown, 11, 56, 58
Boulter, Hugh, Archbishop of
   Armagh, 41
Bourchier, Sir George, 30
Bow Bridge, 15
Bow Street, 24
Bradocke Bridge, 31
Bradock's Brook, 30
Bradogue River, 11, 31
Brangan, Thomas, 57
Brian Boru, 13
Bridewell Bridge, 23
Bridge Gate, 28
Bridge Street, 24
Bridge Street Quay, 16
Broadstone Station, 14, 31, 43
Brookes Quay, 16
Brooking's Map of Dublin, 23,
   34, 35, 38, 47
Browne, Dan, 17
Bruce, Edward, 25
Bruce, Robert, 25
Brunswick Street North, 31
Bull Island, 55-6
Bull Wall, 54, 55
Bullock Harbour, 59
Bunmahon, Co Waterford, 57
Burgh, Thomas, 33
Burgh, William, 18
Burgh Quay, 16, 43
Burghley, Lord, 42
Burgoyne, Colonel John Fox,
   19
Butt, Isaac, 43
Butt Bridge, 43, 44, 47
Byrne, Alfred, 43
Byrne, Edward, Archbishop
   Dublin, 21

Camac River, 11, 13, 15, 23
Camden, Earl of, 48
Canal Docks, 48-9
Capel, Arthur, Earl of Essex,
   34
Capel Street Bridge, 34-6
Cardiff Lane, 20
Cardiff's Lane, 46
Carey, Sir George, 41
Carey's Hospital, 37, 41
Carlisle, Earl of, 40
Carlisle Bridge, 20, 36
Carmelite Order, 31
Carr, John, 24, 26
Carragh, Co Kildare, 6-7
Carson, James, 40
Carton, Co Kildare, 8
Case's Tower, 28
Cassoon, The, 59
Cecil, Sir Robert, 30
Chancery Street, 31

Channel Row, 31
Chapelizod, 9-10
Chapelizod Bridge, 10
Charles I, King, 19, 24
Charles II, King, 14, 19, 22
Charleville Avenue, 48
Chichester, Sir Arthur, 41
Christ Church Cathedral, 25,
   26, 28, 29(p)
Church Street Bridge, 24
Circular Road, 20, 48
Cistercian Order, 24, 31
City Quay, 16, 20, 44
Clanbrassil Street, 32
Clancy Barracks, 15
Clane, Co Kildare, 8
Clar Rade, 57
Clarence Hotel, 33
Clarendon Street, 43
Clarke's Map of Dublin, 24
Clontarf, 47, 59
Clontarf, Battle of, 13, 24
Clontarf, Pool of, 54
Clontarf, Sheds of, 55
Clontarf Island, 50, 54-5
Clontarf Road, 10-11, 55
Coal Quay, 16, 29
Coal Quay Bridge, 27
Coats, William, 39
Cock Lake, 56-7
Cockle Hall, 55
Cockle Point, 55
Cogan, Miles, 38-9
Cogan, Richard, 38-9
Colbert Road, 12
College Green, 20, 36, 38, 41-2
College Park, 46
Collins, Councillor Michael, 45
Collins, General Michael, 18
Collins Barracks, 18
Commons Street, 20
Confederation of Kilkenny, 24
Conniving House, Irishtown,
   53
Connolly Station, 14, 43
Constitution Hill, 31
Conyngham Road, 15
Cook Street, 26
Cookstown, 32
Cooley, Thomas, 25, 46
Corbally, 8
Corporation for Preserving
   and Improving the Port of
   Dublin, 20-1, 47, 49, 59
Crab Lake, 55
Crampton Court, 32
Crampton Quay, 16
Crane, The, 29, 30, 33
Crane Lane, 32
Creighton Street, 20
Cromwell, Christopher, 55
Cromwell, Oliver, 50
Cromwell's Steps, 50
Crosses Quay, 16
Custom House, 5(p), 16, 20,
   27, 33(p), 46, 49, 50
   history of, 44
Custom House Dock, 20
Custom House Docks, 45
Custom House Quay, 16, 32,
   33, 36, 44

Daglish, Robert Jnr, 21

Dalkey, 50
Dame Lane, 36
Dame Street, 32, 38, 39
Dames Gate, 37
Dames Mills, 323
Danes Bridge, 24
de Gomme's Map of Dublin,
   32, 33, 41, 47, 50
De Leuw, Chadwick and
   O hEocha, 44
de Londres, Archbishop Henry,
   46
de Riddelisford, Walter, 39
Denzille Lane, 37
Dewhurst, J C, 15
Dirty Lane, 19
Dr Steevens' Hospital, 15, 17,
   20
Dodder River, 11, 20, 32, 37,
   48, 50
Doherty, W J, 35, 40
D'Olier Street, 15, 36, 40, 43,
   45
Dollard's printing house, 33
Dolly (ship), 36
Dollymount, 55
Dominican Order, 24-5
Doney River, 49
Donney Brook, 49
Donnybrook, 49
Down survey map, 43
Draught of Turleyhydes, The,
   57
Drogheda Street, 40
Droichead Nua, Co Kildare, 7
Droichet Dubhghaill, 24
Dubh Linn, 32
Dublin and Kingstown
   Railway, 15, 43, 56
Dublin Bay, plan of, 56
Dublin Bridge, 24
Dublin Castle, 32
Dublin Corporation, 17
   Paving and Lighting
   Committee, 43-4
Dublin Port and Docks Board,
   16, 44, 47, 49
Dublin Road, 55
Dun Horse Inn, 46
Dunghill Lane, 23
Dunlaoghaire, 56, 58

early timber bridge, 27(p)
East Quay, 17
East Road, 47
East Wall, 17, 47-8, 54
East Wall Road, 47, 50, 54, 55
Easter Rising, 1916, 14, 22-3,
   44
Eastern Franchises, 57
Eastern Health Board, 22
Eastlink Bridge, 20, 47, 51, 52
Eden Quay, 16, 17, 43
Edward II, King, 25
Edward VII, King, 7-8
Electricity Supply Board, 53
Elizabeth I, Queen, 13, 21, 24,
   27, 30, 42, 59
Ellis Quay, 16, 19
Ellis Street, 19
Ellis's Bridge, 23
Emancipation Bridge, 20, 21

Emmet, Robert, 41, 57
Emmet Road, 15
Esmonde, Dr John, 40
Essex Bridge, 19, 27-36, 40
Essex Quay, 16, 28, 29, 33
estuary, pools in, 53-4
Eucharistic Congress, 1932, 40
Evans, Richard, 8
Exchequer Street, 36, 38

Fairview, 47
Fairview Strand, 11
Fassaugh Road, 31
Father Mathew Bridge, 15, 23, 24, 26
ferries, 19-20, 36
Fishamble Street, 28, 29
Fitzgerald, Lord Edward, 22
Fitzgerald, Silken Thomas, 13, 14, 31, 32, 42
Fitzsymon's Tower, 28
Fitzwilliam Square, 35
Fleet Alley, 20
Fleet Street, 11
Food Kitchen, 18-19
Forbes, George, 48
Forbes Castle, 47-8
Forbes Street, 20
Forster, John, 54
Four Courts, 11, 24-6
Fowkes, Nathaniel, 19
Fowler, Richard, 17
Fownes Street, 39
Fox, Charles James, 22
Fox and Geese, 15
Franchises, Eastern, 57
Frank Sherwin Bridge, 17
Friars Bridge, 24
Fyan, Richard, 28
Fyan's Castle, 19, 28, 29, 30
Fysshe Slypp, 19

Gallanstown, 15
gallows, 20, 40
Gandon, James, 25, 40, 42, 44
Garda Siochana, 14
Gardiner's Mall, 40
George Dublin Lighthouse, 59
George I, King
    statue of, 34, 35-6
George IV, King, 17
George's Dock, 45
George's Quay, 16, 20
Gilbert, Sir John, 20, 38, 41
Gillamocholmog, 39
Gloucester Street South, 46
Gogarty, Oliver St John, 12
Golden Falls, 6
Goldenbridge, 15
Goltzius, Hendrik, 57
Grafton Street, 36, 43
Grand Canal, 8, 15, 48
Grand Canal Street, 11, 46
Grangegorman, 31
Grattan, Henry, 22
Grattan Bridge, 19, 28-36, 40
Gravel Walk Slip, 19
graving docks, 49
Gray, Edmund Dwyer, 40
Gray's Ferro-Concrete
    (Ireland) Ltd, 43
Great Britain Quay, 20, 48

Great Brunswick Street, 46
Great Eastern, The (ship), 49
Great Northern Railway, 47
Great South Wall, 36, 50, 52-59
Great Southern and Western
    Railway, 14, 15, 22
Green Patch, The, 52
Gregory, Lady, 36
Griffeen River, 9
Guild Street, 14, 20, 43
Guinness's Brewery, 16, 22, 48
gunpowder explosion, 30

Half Moon Battery, 54, 57, 59
Halpin, George Snr, 16
Halston Street, 31
Handel, George Frederick, 20
Ha'penny Bridge, 16, 20, 20-1, 36
Harcourt, Earl of, 25
Harcourt Street Station, 14
Harcourt Terrace, 43
Harold's Cross, 32
Harrington, General the Earl of, 58
Harrington, Timothy, 53
Harristown, Co Kildare, 6
Hatfield Plan, 42-3
Hawkins, William, 41
Hawkins Quay, 16
Hawkins Street, 19, 22, 41, 43
Hawkins Wall, 43, 46
Helga (ship), 5(p), 44
Henry II, King, 37
Henry III, King, 11
Henry VIII, King, 13, 14, 25, 31, 42
Heuston, Captain Sean, 15, 22-3
Heuston Station, 14, 15, 22, 43
Hibernian Marine School, 20, 46-7
Hibernian Marine Society, 46-7
High Street, 26
HMS Bounty (ship), 59
Hog and Butts, 37
Hogan Place, 46
Hogan's Green, 37
Hoggen Butts, 37
Hoggen Green, 36-9, 41, 42, 46
    Battle of, 38-9
Horse Guards Depot, 32
House of Lords, 42
Howe, The, 37
Howth, 50, 53, 55

Inchicore, 15
Infirmary Road, 11
Inner Dock, 45
Inns Quay, 16, 24, 25, 26
Irish Concrete Society, 17
Irishenco Ltd, 17, 52
Irishtown, 11, 49, 53, 56, 57
Iron Pool, 54
Iron Quay, 16
Island Street, 22, 23
Islandbridge, 11
Islandbridge Memorial Park, 10
Issolde's Tower, 28
Ivory, Thomas, 46
James I, King, 33

James Larkin Road, 55
James's Bridge, 20
James's Street Harbour, 48
Jervis, Sir Humphrey, 27, 31, 34
Jervis' Quay, 16
John, King, 12, 24, 57
John Street, 19
John the Wode, 38, 39
Johnston, Francis, 22, 41
Joyce, James, 6, 10, 55, 57
Joyce, Weston, 9-10

Kilbarrack, 55
Kilcullen, Co Kildare, 7
Kildare, Co
    Liffey in, 6-8
Kildare, Earl of, 31
Kildare, Earls of, 8
Killeen, John, 20
Kilmainham Bridge, 12-13, 15
Kilmainham Gaol, 15
Kilmaston, 12
Kilmehanoc Ford, 11-12, 13, 57
Kimmage, 32
King, Anthony, 33
King John's Bridge, 24
King's Bridge, 15, 17, 18, 20
King's Inns, 25
Kings Inns Quay, 16
King's Mill, 32
Kings River, 6
Kingsbridge Station
    see Heuston Station
Kingstown, 50
Kipling, Rudyard, 19
Kippure Mountain, 6, 49
Knights Hospitallers, 11, 13-14
Knights Templars, 13-14
Knockannavea Mountain, 15
Knowles, George, 24, 26
Kurtz, Messrs, 20

La Touche, John, 6
Lacy Hill, 46
Lacy's drawing, 15
Lambay Catch (ship), 46
Lane, Sir Hugh, 36
Lansdowne Road, 11
Lazers Hill, 16, 37, 38, 42, 45-6
Lazy Hill Walk, 46
Leinster Aqueduct, 8-9
Leixlip, 6, 8-9
Leixlip Bridge, 9
Lennox Street, 43
Liberty Hall, 44
Liffey Bridge, 20
Liffey Meadows, 15
Liffey River
    ancient shore line, 10-11
    in Co Kildare, 6-8
    estuarine pools, 53-4
    ferries, 19-20
    floods, 26
    names of, 6
    source, 6
    into the city, 9-10
Liffey Strand, 12
Liffey Viaduct, 14-15
Lime Street, 20, 46
Lincoln Place, 37
Little John, 24

Loftus, Archbishop, 42
Long Stone, The, 36, 43
Loopline Bridge, 43-4, 50
Lowsie Hill, 46
Lucan, 9
Lucy, Sir Anthony, 57
Luke Kelly Bridge, 47
Lutyens, Sir Edwin, 10, 36

Mabbott, Mr, 19
Mc Carthy and Partners, 50
Mac Murrough, Dermot, 39, 42
McGloughlin, Charles E, 43
Mackey, James W, 40
McSwiney, Peter Paul, 35
Madden, Richard, 57
Magh Maistean, 12
Maiden Tower, 59
Maigneann, St, 13
Mallagh, Joseph, 43
Malton, James, 14, 18, 44, 46
Mansion House, 35
Marine Nursery, 46
Martello Tower, Sandymount, 56
Martello Tower, Seapoint, 58
Martin, Messrs, 20
Martin, T & C, 45
Mary's Abbey
    see St Mary's Abbey
Meetinghouse Lane, 31
Mellowes, Liam, 23
Mellowes Bridge, 19, 23
Memorial Road, 44
Mendicity Institution, 22-3
Merchants Quay, 16, 26
Merchants Road, 47
Merrion Gates, 11, 56
Merrion Square, 43
Merrion Street Upper, 47
Meyler, Thomas, 57
Midland Great Western
    Railway, 9, 48
Millicent Bridge, 8
Milltown, 49
Moira, Dowager Countess of, 22
Moira House, 22-3
Monastery of the Holy Trinity, 37
Moss Street, 20, 44
Mud Island, 48
Murdering Lane, 15

National Gallery of Ireland, 59
National Graves Association, 23
Nelly (ship), 33
New Bridge, Harristown, 6
New Bridge Inn, 7
New Gate, 29
New Port, 49-50
New Wapping Street, 14
Newman, Jacob, 28, 32
Newman's Tower, 28, 32
Niall Glundubh, 12
Nichols Quay, 16
Nimmo, Alexander, 6
Norris, Sir James, 30
North Bull, 55-6
North Lots, 47
North Quay, 16

North Quay Extension, 16, 49
North Strand, 47
North Strand Quay, 17
North Strand Road, 11
North Wall, 14, 20, 45, 47, 48
North Wall Extension, 16, 49
North Wall Quay, 16, 50
Nottingham, Robert, 25

O'Byrnes of Wicklow, 12
Ocean Pier, 49
O'Connell, Daniel, 40
O'Connell Bridge, 16, 20, 36, 40, 55
O'Connell Street, 20, 40
O'Donovan Rossa, Jeremiah, 27
O'Donovan Rossa Bridge, 24, 26-7
O'Dwyer, Frederick, 23
Office of Public Works, 10
O'Kelly, Sean T, 49
Old Bridge, 15, 19, 23, 24, 27(p), 31
Old Custom House, 33
Old Custom House Quay, 16
Old Dock, 44, 45
Old Ferry, 19
Old Four Courts, 25
Old Kilmainham, 15
Old Shore, The, 36, 41-2
Olympia Theatre, 38
O'More, Rory, 21
O'Neill, Sir Phelim, 24
Ordnance Survey Maps, 23
    1837, 15
    1838, 31, 47-8, 57
Ormonde, Duke of, 14
Ormonde Bridge, 26, 27, 29
Ormonde Quay, 11, 16, 31
Ostmans Bridge, 24
Ostmans Gate, 24, 28
Our Lady of Dublin, 31
Oxmantown, 25, 31

Paisley, Jonas, 35
Papworth, George, 17
Parkgate Street, 20
Parliament House, 41
Patent Slip, 49
Pearce, Capt Edward Lovett, 41
Pearse Station, 14, 15, 43
Pearse Street, 45, 46
Pembroke Quay, 16
Peppard, Edward, 37-8
Perrott, Sir John, 27
Perry, Captain John, 55
pesthouses, 55
Petrie, George, 18, 22
Phoenix Iron Works, 9, 17
Phoenix Park, 11, 12, 14, 15, 21
Pidgeon, John, 52
Pigeon House, The, 52-3
Pigeonhouse, 59
Pigeonhouse Fort, 53, 57
Pigeonhouse Hotel, 52-3
Pill Lane, 31
Pimlico Parliament, 44
Poddle River, 11, 16, 28, 32-3, 36
Pollaphuca Bridge, 6
Poolbeg, 54, 56

Poolbeg Electricity Generating Station, 53
Poolbeg Lighthouse, 6, 54, 59
Poolbeg Street, 11, 46
Porter's Row, 19
Portland Row, 20
Post Chaise Companion, 59
Prickett's Tower, 28, 29
Prince of Wales (ship), 57-8
Princes Street, 20
Proudfoot's Castle, 28, 29
Pudding Row, 26, 29
Purcell, Pierce, 43

Quarry Road, 31
quays, 15-17
Queen Maev Bridge, 23
Queen's Bridge, 23

Rathfarnham Water, 49
Rathmines, 47
Rawdon, Sir John, 22
Reinelan, 57
Rennie, John, 45
Revenue Commissioners, 44
Richard II, King, 19
Richmond, Duchess of, 26
Richmond Bridge, 26
Richmond Guard Tower, 21-2
Riding the Franchises, 57
Ringsend, 11, 20, 49, 50, 56-9
Ringsend Point, 19, 20
Ringsend Road, 49
Robinson, William, 14, 25
Rochdale (ship), 57-8
Roche, Tom, 50
Rock Road, 11, 56
Rocque's Maps of Dublin, 18, 19, 23, 39, 47, 49
Rogers, Thomas, 55
Rogerson's Wall, 49
Rory O'More Bridge, 15, 16, 18-23
Royal Artillery Barracks, 15
Royal Barracks, 14, 18, 19
Royal Canal, 8-9, 20, 48
Royal College of Surgeons, 43
Royal Dublin Fusiliers, 45
Royal Hospital, Kilmainham, 15, 22
    hospice, 14
    Knights Hospitallers, 11, 13-14
Russell, Thomas, 22
Rutland, Duke of, 25, 44
Rye Water River, 8

Sadler, William, 59
St Andrew's Church, 37
St Anne's Park, 55
St Augustine Street, 24
St Augustine's Monastery, 37
St James's Bridge, 20
St John's Road, 12
St Mary de Hogges, 37
St Mary on the Bridge, 24
St Mary's Abbey, 10, 31, 34
St Mary's Abbey Quay, 17
St Matthew's Church, Irishtown, 49
St Patrick's Cathedral, 32
St Patrick's Well, 37

St Saviour's Priory, 10, 23, 24-5
St Stephen's Green, 43
St Thomas's Abbey, 32
Sallagh River, 32
Sallcocks Wood, 12
Salmon Pool, 54
Sand Quay, 16
Sandwith Street, 11, 45-6, 49
Sandymount, 56-7
Sarah Bridge, 11, 12-13
Sarsfield Bridge, 17
Sarsfield Quay, 16
Savage, James, 24, 26
Sean Heuston Bridge, 15, 17
Seapoint, 58
Semple, George, 23, 27, 34, 35
Seville Place, 20
Sheds of Clontarf, 55
Shelbourne Road, 49
Sheriff Street, 47, 49
Sherwin, Frank, 17
Sidney, Sir Henry, 13
Silver Street, 19
Sir John Rogerson's Quay, 16, 20, 46
Sirr, Major, 22
Skeffington, Sir William, 13, 14
Skinners Row, 25
Slige Midluachra, 24
slips, 19, 39
Smith, John, 59
Smithfield Market, 19
Smoothing Iron, 55
Smyth, Edward, 27, 40, 44
Smyth, John, 27
South Bank Quay, 16
South Bull, 49, 50, 56-7, 57, 58
South Circular Road, 15, 22
South Lots Road, 46, 49
South Quay, 16
South Wall, 20, 54
Soyer, Alexis, 18-19
Speed's Map of Dublin, 28, 29, 31, 32, 38, 41, 42, 43
Spencer Dock, 48
Stanihurst, Richard, 28
Steadfast Dick, 36
Stein River, 16, 36, 41-3, 45
Stoney, Bindon, 35, 40, 49
Strand Road, 11, 56
Strawberry Beds, 9
Strongbow, 13, 39
Suffolk Street, 36, 37
Summer Islands, 11
Sutton, 55
Sutton Creek, 55
Swift, Dean Jonathan, 8, 20
Swift's Row, 32, 36
Swivel Bridge, 43

Table Mountain, 6
Talbot, Venerable Matt, 44-5
Talbot Memorial Bridge, 16, 44-5
Talbot Street, 11
Tallaght, 32
Tandy, Napper, 44
Temple Bar, 19, 39
Temple Lane, 19, 41
Thackeray, William Makepeace, 35-5
Thingmount, The, 36-7, 39

Thomas Street, 11
Thorncastle, 50
Tolka Quay, 50, 54
Tolka River, 31, 47, 55
    estuary, 11
Tone, Theobald Wolfe, 8, 22
towers, 27-8
Townsend Street, 45, 46
Trinity College, 36, 37, 42-3, 46
Tudor's Drawing of Dublin, 33
Tunstal family, 52

United Irishmen, 53
University of Birmingham, 36
Usher, Arnold, 23
Usher, John, 49
Usher, Sir William, 49
Usher's Island, 16, 21, 22-3, 28
Usher's Pill, 23, 24
Usher's Quay, 16, 23

Vallancey, Charles, 23
van Nost, John, the Elder, 35
Vesey, Agmondisham, 9
Victoria, Queen, 7, 21
Victoria Bridge, 20
Victoria Quay, 16
Vignoles, Charles, 15

Walsh, William, 36
Walsh, William (yeoman), 57
Wapping Street, 20
Warren, Robert, 35
watermills, 15, 32-3
Watling Street, 21
Watling Street Bridge, 20
Wellesley, Marquis, 17
Wellington Bridge, 36
Wellington Quay, 16, 39
Wesley, John, 20, 22
Westland Row, 45
Westland Row Station
    see Pearse Station
Westmoreland, Countess of, 12
Westmoreland Street, 11, 15, 20, 36, 40
Whitefriar Street, 31
White's Quay, 16
Whitworth, Earl of, 24
Whitworth Bridge, 24
Wicklow, Co. Liffey in, 6
Wide Streets Commissioners, 24
William of Aier (ship), 54
William of Orange, King, 18
William Street South, 39
William Usher's House, 28
Wine, Warden, 46
Winetavern Street, 26, 27, 28, 29
Woffington, Peg, 20
Wolfe Tone Quay, 16, 18
Wood, Sancton, 15
Wood Quay, 10, 11, 16, 26-30
    gunpowder explosion, 30
Woodham-Smith, Cecil, 18
Woolpack Road, 7

Yeats, William Butler, 36
Young Ireland movement, 53

Zozimus, 34-5